NUTRICIA

The
Wheat-
AND
Gluten-free
Cookbook

NUTRICIA

The

Wheat-

AND

Gluten-free

Cookbook

Joan Noble

VERMILION
LONDON

Text © Nutricia Dietary Products
Photography © Ebury Press

First printed in 1993 by Vermilion,
an imprint of Ebury Press, Random House,
20 Vauxhall Bridge Road, London SW1V 2SA.

Random House Australia (Pty) Limited
20 Alfred Street, Milsons Point, Sydney,
New South Wales 2061, Australia.

EDITED AND COMPILED BY Donna Wood and Julia Canning
DESIGNED BY Terry Jeavons
PHOTOGRAPHY BY James Murphy

Random House UK Limited Reg. No. 954009

A CIP catalogue record for this book is available
from the British Library.

ISBN 0 09 177998 7

Printed in Great Britain by Mackays of Chatham

CONTENTS

INTRODUCTION

～～

All kinds of people may, at one time or another, want to exclude foods that contain gluten, a protein found in wheat, rye, barley and oats, from their diet. Others may have an intolerance to wheat. This could be because they suffer from certain allergies, or perhaps they have discovered that they feel unwell after eating bread or flour-based dishes. By doing without these foods for a while, they hope to detect some improvement in their general well-being.

A large number of people have tried gluten-free or wheat-free diets for a variety of conditions and found that they alleviate their symptoms although there may or may not be scientific evidence to support this.

Coeliac disease

By far the largest group of people who are required to follow a gluten-free diet are coeliacs, of which it is estimated there are between forty and fifty thousand in the UK. A medical definition of coeliac disease is a permanent intolerance to gluten, whereby there is damage to the small intestine which improves when treated with a gluten-free diet. Symptoms can include diarrhoea, weight loss, mouth ulcers, anaemia and vitamin deficiencies. Many people may be coeliacs without any symptoms at all, although damage to the small intestine has already occurred. Other people may have less-common symptoms. A lot of research in this area is currently underway. Dermatitis herpetiformis is a related condition in which there is a skin rash from which the majority of patients show an improvement on a gluten-free diet. Other conditions such as diabetes have also been associated with coeliac disease.

Coeliac disease is derived from the Greek word *koiliakos* which means 'suffering in the bowels'. The condition was first described in the second century AD in the writings of a Roman physician who also claimed that bread was not suitable for these patients. However it was not until the late-nineteenth century that Dr Samuel Gee of St Bartholomew's Hospital in London gave the second classic description of coeliac disease.

Early this century a few physicians drew attention to the harmful effects of carbohydrates and a diet low in carbohydrates was recommended. However, no real progress in treating the disease was made until 1950. Professor Dicke, a Dutch paediatrician, found that wheat and rye flour cause the symptoms of coeliac disease. This led to the recommendation that coeliacs should live on a diet free of wheat and rye.

The emergence of gluten-free products

In those early days only a few products made with gluten-free flour were available on the market, so coeliacs gave up flour-based dishes and turned to the foods which contain no gluten, such as fruit, vegetables, nuts, pulses, seeds, oils, margarine, meat, fish and dairy produce. The emergence of support groups such as the Coeliac Society of Great Britain soon instigated the call for greater understanding of the disease and better provision for its members.

The first bakery dedicated to gluten-free foods was set up in the 1950s by a company now part of Nutricia. At this stage the loaves produced were a very poor substitute for 'real' bread and were presented in round tins. In the early 80s a breakthrough was made into producing vacuum-packed bread that looked and tasted more like normal bread. Nutricia now has the largest gluten-free bakery in the world, in Stockport near Manchester, purpose-built to cater for the needs of people on special diets. At the same time a wide range of other gluten-free foods was developed to include crackers, cakes, biscuits and flour mixes.

Wheat-free or gluten-free?

Coeliacs can differ widely in their sensitivity to gluten. As some of the gluten-free products currently available are actually prepared from wheatstarch and therefore contain minute amounts of gluten, they could represent some danger to a minority of very sensitive patients. This could be side-stepped by a wider use of 100 per cent wheatstarch-free products, based on naturally gluten-free flour such as maize, soya or rice. All the recipes in this book are based on naturally gluten-free starches and ingredients and therefore can be followed with full confidence for all coeliacs and others who suffer from wheat intolerance.

The main aim of this book is to make sure that those people who are on a wheat or gluten-free diet do not feel the need to cheat or stray from it. Some may be able to tolerate small amounts of wheat or gluten without feeling ill in the short term, but if they continue to cheat on their prescribed diet they may find that serious consequences such as anaemia, weak bones and vitamin deficiencies will result.

A quick look at the delicious recipes that follow should be enough to strengthen even the weakest of wills, but many people told by their doctor to exclude wheat and/or gluten from their diet will admit an initial reaction of horror. How, they wonder, is it possible to live a normal life without any of the everyday foods that we all take for granted? What substitute can there possibly be for good old bread, pies and cakes?

The answer is that as well as the ready made gluten-free flours and mixes available from companies like Nutricia, there is also quite a large number of substitutes for wheat flour.

A list of the better-known ones follows – your local health-food shop should stock most, if not all of them.

Rice flour Excellent in puddings, biscuits and cakes.

Maize flour Also known as cornmeal, maize can be used in bread, cakes and biscuits as well as for thickening.

Soya flour Made from ground soya beans, it is a source of protein, fat and B vitamins.

Gram flour Often found in Indian dishes, it is made from ground chickpeas and is high in nutritional value.

Buckwheat flour This flour has a superb binding quality and is rich in B vitamins and protein.

Arrowroot A useful thickening agent for sauces, gravies and casseroles.

Sago, millet and tapioca These are also suitable ingredients for thickening and useful in puddings.

A combination of starches often works better than one on its own.

Following a special diet depends a great deal on careful shopping. The contents of your nearest wholefood or health food shop may appear offputting and unfamiliar at first, but a little experimentation will open up many new possibilities. At the supermarket, look out for the crossed grain of wheat sign on tins and packets. This sign is an international symbol indicating that the food is gluten-free. Always read manufacturer's labels with care, as sometimes complicated terms such as 'modified starch' are used and need to be checked.

Some of the most unlikely foods are found to be harbouring gluten or wheat in their list of ingredients. Products such as soy sauce, mixed spices, salad dressings, English mustard, stock cubes and gravy mixes which may seem quite innocent, can represent danger for anyone who cannot tolerate gluten or wheat, as well as commercially prepared sausages, beefburgers, pâtés, fish in batter or breadcrumbs, some processed cheese spreads, yoghurts and malted milk drinks. Even baked beans, soups and dry-roasted nuts cannot always be trusted! To help you through the minefield, the major supermarket chains offer a very useful service to their customers, supplying on request a list of their own-brand foods which are completely gluten-free. Request up-to-date information as the manufacturers do change their recipes.

Compliance with a special diet

Keeping rigidly to a diet which excludes some of the most popular and widely available foods can be hard, especially outside the home or in social situations. Many factors affect a person's ability to maintain serious changes in their diet – their interest in food in general, their personality type, whether they live alone or as part of a large family, what the canteen facilities are like at work, school or college and whether they or someone else does the shopping and cooking. Coeliac diabetics have extra problems, because as well as making sure all the food they eat is gluten-free, they also have other dietary restrictions.

A working mum who is herself a diagnosed coeliac may find it difficult to find the time and energy to shop diligently for gluten-free ingredients and cook herself separate meals from the rest of the family. Older children may want to eat at friends' houses or join in the fun at the local fast food venues, but feel too self-conscious to explain about their condition for fear of drawing attention to themselves. Teenagers often rebel against their diet because the desire to do as their peers do is so strong.

People whose jobs involve a lot of entertaining may find restaurant menus daunting as they are unsure what they are 'allowed' to eat. They may play safe by choosing basic plain foods such as grills and fruit. The cost of following a gluten-free or wheat-free diet can also be an issue, although the money saved on pre-packaged convenience foods such as cakes, pies and so on will buy more of the better-value healthy, naturally gluten-free foods such as meat, fish, chicken, fruit and vegetables recommended for everyone.

To alleviate some of these difficulties, the recipes on the following pages are composed of good, wholesome ingredients designed to appeal to all members of the family, even if only one cannot tolerate wheat or gluten. Many are based around the type of food people on a wheat or gluten-free diet would normally have to avoid, such as goujons of sole or chicken drumsticks covered in breadcrumbs, taramasalata and all kinds of cakes and pastry dishes made with special wheat-flour replacers.

It is essential that friends and family members show support to the person with a food intolerance and help them to stick to their diet without being made to feel the odd one out. For this reason the recipes presented here embrace family meals, packed lunches, picnics and snacks. As many of the meals are interchangeable within each section there is something for every occasion. With a little care and imagination, a wheat-free and gluten-free diet can appeal to everyone, as this book sets out to show.

Many of the recipes are based around Nutricia's wheat- and gluten-free products, all of which are available from chemists and selected health food stores. If you do not see these products on the shelves, ask for them – they can easily be ordered for you. Some can also be obtained on prescription for medically diagnosed coeliacs and those with dermatitis herpetiformis. And as Nutricia's range of gluten-free breads, versatile mixes, pasta, cakes and biscuits is now available in more than ten different countries, holidays abroad should no longer pose any problems for coeliacs and others.

Healthy eating for all

Over the last twenty years or so, there has been a tremendous surge in public awareness that 'we are what we eat'. The general consensus of opinion is that most people eat too much fat, salt and sugar and too little fibre and starch. A healthy diet is a balanced diet which contains fats, proteins, carbohydrates and energy in the correct proportions and is rich in vitamins, minerals, trace elements, essential fatty acids and fibre.

Medical and nutritional experts now seem united in the belief that the kind of food eaten by people in the Mediterranean countries is one of the healthiest options for all of us, whether we suffer from food intolerances or not. A typical Mediterranean diet includes plenty of fruit and vegetables which are rich in antioxidants such as vitamins C and E, starchy foods like bread and pasta, fresh fish, some meat and olive oil.

General tips for a healthy diet

● It is a good idea to use pulses like kidney beans, haricot beans, chick peas and lentils as high-protein, low-fat alternatives to meat. When using meat, choose the leanest cuts and trim off all visible fat before cooking.

● Try to eat more white meat such as chicken or turkey. Limit the amount of beef, pork and offal during a week. Try to eat a portion of oily fish rich in polyunsaturates (such as mackerel, salmon, tuna and herring) at least twice a week.

● As anyone who cannot eat wheatflour and its products automatically forfeits its high-fibre value, fibre must be brought into the diet in other ways. Increase your intake of foods such as soya bran, rice bran, beet fibre, beans, brown rice, jacket potatoes and fresh fruit and vegetables with the skins on. You could also add Nutricia's gluten-free high fibre flour mix to recipes where appropriate.

● Cook with olive oil and/or polyunsaturated oils such as sunflower, corn etc., instead of lard, hydrogenated margarine or cooking oil, to help lower blood cholesterol and improve general health.

● Be sure to eat regularly – ideally three well-balanced meals a day.

● Cut down on alcohol, especially spirits. Recent research suggests red wine can be good for you in moderation!

Using the recipes

The recipes that follow are designed to be used year in, year out, for everyday meals as well as celebratory occasions, so ideas for adapting them, to 'ring the changes' are often given. In most cases we have cut down on full-fat cheese quantities, often substituting low-fat cheese, fromage frais or Greek yoghurt for cream, and used olive oil or polyunsaturated oil instead of saturated fat, but here and there butter has been used for flavour and you will find a smattering of 'naughty but nice' ingredients for use on high days and holidays or when entertaining. As with all things, moderation is the key!

For your information, each of the recipes has been given a nutritional analysis to determine exactly the amount of energy, protein, fat and carbohydrate it contains, per portion. All spoon measurements are based on standard measures – 1 teaspoon equals 5ml, 1 tablespoon equals 15ml. Egg size is medium/size 3 unless otherwise stated. Always follow either the metric or imperial measurements, never mix the two, and follow the instructions carefully. Remember that no two ovens are the same, so the cooking times may vary slightly from that stated.

We believe that if you are new to life on a wheat-or gluten-free diet you can take heart at the tasty and varied dishes in this cookbook. It is our hope that, armed with a greater knowledge of your condition and the courage to experiment with some perhaps unfamiliar ingredients, it will equip you with a diet plan for life and convince you that a healthy eating regime that excludes wheat and gluten can be fun, challenging and open new doors.

For further information write to:
Nutricia Dietary Products Limited
494-496 Honeypot Lane Stanmore Middlesex HA7 1JR

STARTERS

CLASSIC MINESTRONE SOUP

SERVES 6

A WONDERFULLY NOURISHING soup from Italy, Minestrone makes a substantial starter, ideal to serve before a light-weight main meal. For the best flavour use really fresh vegetables - they can be varied according to season and availability. You might like to include long-grain rice instead of the pasta.

INGREDIENTS

75 g (3 oz) cannellini beans
15 ml (1 tbs) olive oil
2 rashers streaky bacon, chopped
1 onion, chopped
1 potato, diced
1 leek, sliced
1 carrot, diced
2 celery sticks, chopped
1/4 green cabbage, shredded
400 g (14 oz) can chopped tomatoes
1.5L (2 1/2 pts) vegetable
or chicken stock

30 ml (2 tbs) tomato purée
1 bay leaf
5 ml (1 tsp) dried mixed herbs
salt and freshly ground black pepper
50 g (2 oz) wheat-free
macaroni or spaghetti
25 g (2 oz) Parmesan cheese,
finely grated

1 Cover the beans in boiling water and leave to soak for 1 hour.

2 Heat the oil in a large saucepan. Add the bacon and onion and cook for 5 minutes, stirring, until lightly browned. Add the potato, leek, carrot, celery and cabbage and continue to cook for 2 minutes, stirring all the time. Add the tomatoes, stock, tomato purée, herbs and drained beans to the pan, then season to taste with salt and pepper. Bring to the boil, then lower the heat and simmer for about 1 1/4 hours.

3 Add the pasta to the pan and continue to simmer for 8 minutes until the pasta is tender. Adjust the seasoning and remove the bay leaf. To serve, spoon into individual bowls and sprinkle with Parmesan cheese.

NUTRITIONAL INFORMATION (PER SERVING)
Energy 523 kJ/125 kcal ▪ *Protein 5 g* ▪ *Carbohydrate 13 g* ▪ *Fat 6 g*

FRESH BEANSPROUTS ADD an oriental touch to this delicate chicken soup. Use the beansprouts on the day of purchase, or store them in the refrigerator overnight and use the next day. Never keep fresh beansprouts for longer than two days as they deteriorate quickly, becoming lifeless and discoloured.

CHICKEN BEANSPROUT SOUP

SERVES 6

INGREDIENTS

15 ml (1 tbs) vegetable oil
1 onion, chopped
25 g (1 oz) button mushrooms, sliced
15 ml (1 tbs) cornflour
1 L (1 ³/4 pt) chicken stock
110 g (4 oz) cooked chicken, cubed

110 g (4 oz) sweetcorn kernels,
canned or frozen
225 g (8 oz) beansprouts, rinsed
1 egg, beaten
15 ml (1 tbs) finely chopped parsley
salt and freshly ground pepper

1 Heat the oil in a large saucepan, add the onion and cook for 3 minutes until softened. Add the mushrooms and continue to cook for 3 minutes. Add the cornflour and stir in the chicken stock, adding slowly at first. Bring to the boil, then reduce to a simmer.

2 Add the diced chicken to the pan, together with the sweetcorn and beansprouts and cook for 10 minutes.

3 Remove a few tablespoons of the soup to a small bowl and combine with the beaten egg. Just before serving, return the egg mixture to the hot soup, stirring briskly. Add the parsley and season to taste with salt and pepper. Serve at once.

NUTRITIONAL INFORMATION (PER SERVING)
Energy 480 kJ/115 kcal ■ Protein 8 g ■ Carbohydrate 10 g ■ Fat 5 g

LAYERED VEGETABLE TERRINE

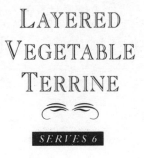

SERVES 6

A VERY ELEGANT starter, this sophisticated-looking terrine is made up of layers of creamy puréed vegetables and can be served hot or cold. Crisp Melba toast is the ideal accompaniment. To make the toast, split a slice of toasted wheat-free bread through the centre with a sharp knife, then toast the uncooked sides under the grill until crisp and curled.

INGREDIENTS

225 g (8 oz) carrots	2 eggs, separated
225 g (8 oz) spinach	salt and freshly ground black pepper
225 g (8 oz) cauliflower	2.5ml (1/2 tsp) ground coriander
50 g (2 oz) margarine	1.5 ml (1/4 tsp) freshly
50 g (2 oz) cornflour	grated nutmeg
300 ml (10 fl oz) milk	

1 Cook the vegetables in separate saucepans of water until tender. Drain well and purée the vegetables separately in a blender or food processor until smooth.

2 Preheat the oven to 180°C/350°F/Gas 4.

3 Melt the margarine in a saucepan, then stir in the cornflour. Remove from the heat and gradually stir in the milk. Return to the heat and simmer, stirring, until the sauce has thickened. Remove from the heat and when slightly cooled, add the egg yolks. Season to taste with salt and pepper. In a separate bowl, whisk the egg white until it forms soft peaks. Gently fold into the sauce.

4 Divide the sauce between the vegetable purées. Season the carrot purée with ground coriander and the spinach with nutmeg and more pepper. Spread the cauliflower purée in the base of a loaf tin. Cover with the spinach purée and then the carrot mixture. Stand in a roasting tin half filled with hot water and bake for about 1 hour until set firm.

5 Leave to stand for 10 minutes, then turn out onto a warmed serving dish. Spoon the yoghurt over the terrine and sprinkle with snipped chives. Slice to serve.

NUTRITIONAL INFORMATION (PER SERVING)
Energy 765 kJ/183 kcal ∎ Protein 7 g ∎ Carbohydrate 15 g ∎ Fat 11 g

LENTILS ARE GOOD news for healthy eating, since they are extremely high in protein and fibre yet low in fat. Flavoured with herbs and orange they make a delicious pâté - serve with a refreshing fruity salad and triangles of toasted wheat-free bread or crackers for a hearty starter or a light lunch.

LENTIL PATE WITH ORANGE SALAD

SERVES 6

INGREDIENTS

250 g (9 oz) split red lentils	*15 ml (3 tsp) tomato purée*
600 ml (1 pt) vegetable stock	*10 ml (2 tsp) dried mixed herbs*
juice of 1/2 orange	*salt and freshly ground black pepper*
1 onion, finely chopped	*25 g (1 oz) margarine or butter, diced*

ORANGE SALAD

2 oranges	*15 ml (1 tbs) orange juice*
175 g (6 oz) fresh spinach leaves	*5 ml (1 tsp) sugar*
1 head of chicory	*salt and freshly ground black pepper*
15 ml (1 tbs) olive oil	*15 ml (1 tbs) chopped pistachio nuts*

1 Spread the lentils on a plate and pick out any bits of grit or discoloured lentils, then place in a sieve and rinse well under cold running water.

2 Place the lentils in a large saucepan with the stock, orange juice, onion, tomato purée and herbs. Season to taste with salt and pepper. Bring to the boil, stirring, then reduce the heat slightly. Simmer for about 30 minutes, stirring frequently, until the lentils are soft and the stock has been absorbed. If the lentils begin to stick to the pan add a little water.

3 Remove from the heat and add the margarine, blending until well incorporated. Leave to cool for about 20 minutes. If a smooth pâté is preferred, work the mixture in a blender or food processor. Adjust the seasoning, spoon into a serving dish and chill for at least 2 hours.

4 To make the salad, remove the peel and pith from the oranges, then cut out the segments, discarding the membranes. Wash the spinach and discard any thick stalks; tear into pieces. Slice the chicory thinly. Combine the orange segments, spinach and chicory in a bowl. Blend the oil with the orange juice and sugar. Season to taste with salt and pepper and pour over the salad. Toss and sprinkle with the pistachio nuts. Serve the salad with the pâté.

NUTRITIONAL INFORMATION (PER SERVING)
Energy 975 kJ/233 kcal ■ Protein 12 g ■ Carbohydrate 30 g ■ Fat 8 g

GUACAMOLE WITH CRISPY DIPPERS

~ ~

SERVES 6

SERVED WITH CRUNCHY potato skins, this tasty Mexican dip is perfect for handing round with pre-dinner drinks. Why not offer a tequila-based cocktail to get the evening off to a wild start!

Take care when preparing the fresh chilli, since it contains a pungent oil which can burn. As a low-fat alternative to the potato dippers, serve the guacamole with sticks of fresh vegetables.

INGREDIENTS

2 ripe avocados
juice of 1 lime
2 tomatoes, skinned and chopped
1/2 green chilli, de-seeded
and finely chopped

1 garlic clove, crushed
2 spring onions, finely chopped
15 ml (1 tbs) finely chopped parsley
2.5 ml (1/2 tsp) ground coriander
salt and freshly ground black pepper

CRISPY DIPPERS
4 large potatoes
45 ml (3 tbs) vegetable oil
salt and freshly ground black pepper

1 To prepare the crispy dippers, boil the potatoes for 15 minutes until just soft. Preheat the oven to 200°C/400°F/Gas 6. Cut each potato into 6 wedges, then scoop out and discard all but a thin layer of flesh. Put the skin shells in a roasting tin, drizzle over the oil and season with salt and pepper. Bake in the oven for about an hour until crisp.

2 To make the dip, halve the avocados, remove the stones and scoop the flesh into a bowl. Add the lime juice and mush until fairly smooth. Add the chopped tomatoes, green chilli, garlic, spring onions, parsley and coriander and mix well. Season to taste with salt and pepper. Cover with cling film if not using immediately.

3 Turn the dip into a serving bowl. Place on a platter and surround with the crispy dippers.

NUTRITIONAL INFORMATION (PER SERVING)
Energy 820 kJ/196 kcal ■ Protein 3 g ■ Carbohydrate 13 g ■ Fat 15 g

MAKE YOUR OWN wheat-free version of this popular Greek dip and serve it in the traditional way, with slices of hot pitta bread. You might like to accompany it with Hummus, another Greek dip.

TARAMASALATA

SERVES 6

INGREDIENTS

4 slices wheat-free bread	*150 ml (5 fl oz) olive oil*
110 g (4 oz) smoked cod's roe, skinned	*12 black olives,*
45 ml (3 tbs) lemon juice	*6 lemon wedges,*
1 garlic clove, crushed	*6 fresh coriander sprigs, to garnish*

1 Remove the crusts from the bread and discard. Cube the bread.

2 Place the cod's roe, bread, lemon juice and garlic in a blender or food processor and blend for 10-15 seconds, until smooth. Scrape down the bowl halfway through processing, if necessary.

3 With the motor running, slowly pour the oil through the feed tube and blend for about 1 second to mix well.

4 Spoon onto individual plates and garnish each portion with 2 olives, a lemon wedge and a coriander sprig.

NUTRITIONAL INFORMATION (PER SERVING)
Energy 1160 kJ/277 kcal ■ *Protein 5 g* ■ *Carbohydrate 6 g* ■ *Fat 26 g*

HAM AND WATERCRESS MOUSSE

SERVES 6

ENHANCE THE SUBTLE colouring of this delicate-tasting mousse with a flowery garnish of radish lilies and watercress sprigs. To make the lily shape, slice through the top of the radish, cutting almost to the base. Cut across to make quarters, then halve again into eights. Place in ice-cold water.

INGREDIENTS

1/2 bunch of watercress
110 g (4 oz) low-fat soft cheese
10 ml (2 tsp) powdered gelatine
150 ml (5 fl oz) cold chicken stock
110 ml (4 fl oz) mayonnaise
175 g (6 oz) cooked ham, minced

1-2 drops Tabasco sauce
freshly ground black pepper
2 egg whites
vegetable oil, for greasing
watercress sprigs and
radish lilies, to garnish

1 Grease an 850 ml (1 1/2 pt) soufflé dish, line the base with greaseproof paper, then lightly grease the paper.

2 Wash and drain the watercress, then remove the stalks. Blanch in boiling water for a few seconds, then drain and refresh under running water. Drain well and transfer to a food processor. Add the cheese and blend until the watercress is finely chopped.

3 Sprinkle the gelatine over the stock in a small pan and leave for a few minutes to soften. Heat gently until dissolved, then cool by standing in a pan of cold water.

4 Stir the gelatine into the watercress mixture, followed by the mayonnaise, ham and Tabasco sauce. Season with pepper. Whisk the egg whites until they stand in stiff peaks, then fold into the mixture. Pour into the prepared soufflé dish and chill for 3 hours until set.

5 To serve, dip the base of the dish in very hot water then turn out onto a serving plate and carefully peel off the lining paper. Garnish with watercress sprigs and radish lilies.

NUTRITIONAL INFORMATION (PER SERVING)
Energy 498 kJ/120 kcal ■ Protein 8 g ■ Carbohydrate 3 g ■ Fat 9 g

START A MEAL on an exotic note with skewers of marinated pork served with a spicy peanut sauce. Cool cucumber makes a refreshing garnish - add a few thin slices of de-seeded green chilli and a sprinkling of lemon juice and sugar to create an instant relish.

INDONESIAN PORK SATAY

SERVES 6

INGREDIENTS

450 g (1 lb) pork fillet
1 garlic clove, crushed
10 ml (2 tsp) grated fresh root ginger
2.5 ml ($^1/2$ tsp) ground coriander
2.5 ml ($^1/2$ tsp) ground turmeric
1.5 ml ($^1/4$ tsp) chilli powder

15 ml (1 tbs) tamari or gluten-free soy sauce
15 ml (1 tbs) peanut oil
15 ml (1 tbs) lemon juice
5 ml (1 tsp) dark soft brown sugar
cucumber twists, to garnish

PEANUT SAUCE

110 g (4 oz) desiccated coconut
300 ml (10 fl oz) hot water
110 g (4 oz) salted peanuts, ground
2.5 ml ($^1/2$ tsp) turmeric powder

$^1/4$ teaspoon chilli powder
15 ml (1 tbs) dark soft brown sugar
5 ml (1 tsp) lemon juice

1 Cut the pork into bite-sized pieces and place in a bowl. Add the garlic, ginger, spices, tamari sauce, oil, lemon juice and sugar. Stir well, then leave to marinate in a cool place for 2 hours, turning the meat occasionally.

2 Meanwhile make the sauce. Put the coconut in a bowl and pour over the hot water. Squeeze the coconut between your fingers for a couple of minutes, then strain into a small saucepan, pressing all the liquid out of the coconut. Discard the coconut. Add the peanuts to the coconut milk with the turmeric, chilli powder and sugar. Bring to the boil then simmer for 2 minutes, stirring constantly. Add the lemon juice and remove from heat.

3 Heat the grill to high. Thread the pork pieces onto 8 thin skewers and brush with the marinade. Grill the satay for 12-15 minutes, turning and basting occasionally with more marinade until cooked through.

4 Serve the satay with the peanut sauce and garnish with cucumber twists.

NUTRITIONAL INFORMATION (PER SERVING)
Energy 1485 kJ/355 kcal ▪ *Protein 21 g* ▪ *Carbohydrate 5 g* ▪ *Fat 28 g*

SESAME PRAWN TOASTS

MAKES 20

A CHINESE RESTAURANT favourite, these crisp prawn-flavoured triangles are wonderful served as an appetizer with dry white wine. Present them garnished with spring onion tassels. To make the tassels, trim the tops and the bulb ends, then remove the skin. Make several slits down the length of each onion, then place in a bowl of iced water for an hour.

INGREDIENTS

225 g (8 oz) uncooked prawns
2 eggs, separated
10 ml (2 tsp) anchovy essence
salt and freshly ground black pepper
10 thin slices wheat-free bread,
crusts removed

15 ml (1 tbs) milk
40 g (1 1/2 oz) sesame seeds
vegetable oil, for frying

1 Place the prawns, egg whites and anchovy essence in a blender or food processor. Season with salt and pepper, and work to a smooth paste. Spread the prawn mixture over 5 slices of bread. Cover with the remaining slices and press the edges down well. Cut each sandwich into 4 triangles.

2 Pour oil into a large frying-pan to a depth of 1 cm (1/2 in) and heat until a stale bread cube browns in 50 seconds.

3 In a bowl, beat the egg yolks with the milk. Dip the prawn triangles into the egg mixture, then sprinkle with sesame seeds.

4 Shallow fry the prawn triangles in the hot oil until golden brown. Drain on absorbent kitchen paper and serve hot.

NUTRITIONAL INFORMATION (PER SERVING)
Energy 375 kJ/90 kcal ■ Protein 4 g ■ Carbohydrate 10 g ■ Fat 4 g

TINY CHEESE-FLAVOURED choux buns, filled with a creamy smoked salmon mixture, make a delectable starter or cocktail nibble. If wished, the smoked salmon can be substituted with another flavoursome fish such as smoked trout, cooked prawns or smoked mackerel.

SALMON CHEESE PUFFS

MAKES 15

INGREDIENTS

150 ml (5 fl oz) water
50 g (2 oz) margarine
65 g (2 1/2 oz) Rite-Diet Flour Mix
pinch of salt
2 eggs, well beaten

15 g (1/2 oz) finely grated
Parmesan cheese
2.5 ml (1/2 tsp) Dijon mustard
fresh parsley sprigs, to garnish

FILLING

110 ml (4 fl oz) low fat cream cheese
5 ml (1 tsp) tomato purée
5 ml (1 tsp) lemon juice

freshly ground black pepper
110 g (4 oz) smoked salmon
trimmings

1 Preheat the oven to 220°C/425°F/Gas 7. Grease a baking tray.

2 Bring the water to the boil in a saucepan. Add the margarine and boil until the margarine has melted. Remove from the heat and immediately stir in all the Flour Mix and salt. Beat well, until the mixture forms a smooth ball, leaving the sides of the pan clean.

3 Allow to cool slightly, then gradually beat in the egg, a little at a time, until the paste is smooth and glossy. Beat in the cheese and mustard.

4 Place heaped teaspoons of the paste on the prepared baking sheet and bake for about 20-25 minutes until well risen and golden. Make a small slit in the side of each puff and leave to cool on a wire rack.

5 Meanwhile, prepare the filling. Mix the cream cheese with the tomato purée and lemon juice, and season with pepper. Chop half of the smoked salmon and stir into the filling. Cut the rest into small strips.

6 Cut open the cold puffs and fill with the cream mixture, topped with strips of salmon. Garnish with parsley sprigs and serve.

NUTRITIONAL INFORMATION (PER SERVING)
Energy 320 kJ/76 kcal ▪ *Protein 4 g* ▪ *Carbohydrate 4 g* ▪ *Fat 5 g*

GOUJONS OF SOLE

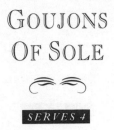

SERVES 4

LITTLE STRIPS OF sole with a crunchy coating make a melt-in-the-mouth start to any meal and will also go down well with children. For a variation in flavour, add a little paprika to the seasoned flour.

To make the breadcrumbs, dry the bread in the oven, then work in a food processor.

INGREDIENTS

500 g (1 lb) sole fillets
50 g (2 oz) wheat-free flour
salt and freshly ground black pepper
50 g (2 oz) dry wheat-free breadcrumbs
1 egg, beaten
30 ml (2 tbs) sunflower oil
fresh parsley sprigs and
lemon wedges, to granish

DIPPING SAUCE
15 ml (1 tbs) chopped gherkins
15 ml (1 tbs) snipped chives
15 ml (1 tbs) capers
5 ml (1 tsp) lemon juice
150 ml (5 fl oz) mayonnaise
freshly ground black pepper

1 Skin the sole and cut into thin strips, about 5 cm (2 in) long, and pat dry with absorbent kitchen paper. Place the flour in a polythene bag and season with salt and pepper. Add the fish and shake the bag until the strips are coated. Spread the crumbs out on a plate. Dip the strips into the egg, then press into the crumbs to coat, shaking off the excess crumbs.

2 Heat the oil a large frying-pan and fry the strips for 4-5 minutes until golden brown. Remove with slotted spoon and drain on absorbent kitchen paper.

3 To make the sauce, stir the gherkins, chives, capers and lemon juice into the mayonnaise. Season to taste with pepper.

4 Arrange the hot goujons on individual plates and garnish with parsley and lemon wedges. Spoon a little sauce onto each plate for dipping.

NUTRITIONAL INFORMATION (PER SERVING)
Energy 2185 kJ/522 kcal ■ Protein 25 g ■ Carbohydrate 14 g ■ Fat 41 g

CRAB IN A CREAMY sauce with a gratin topping makes a quick starter - and tastes sensational!

For an interesting garnish, finely chop separately the whites and yolks of two hard-boiled eggs and 30 ml (2 tbs) parsley. Arrange in alternate lines of white, yellow and green.

DEVILLED CRAB RAMEKINS

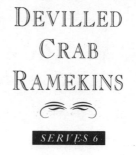

SERVES 6

INGREDIENTS

350 g (12 oz) frozen crabmeat, defrosted
300 ml (10 fl oz) fromage frais
5 ml (1 tsp) Worcestershire sauce
5 ml (1 tsp) Dijon mustard
30 ml (2 tbs) medium sherry

pinch of cayenne pepper
salt and freshly ground black pepper
90 ml (6 tbs) fresh wheat-free breadcrumbs
30 ml (2 tbs) finely grated Parmesan cheese
40 g (1 1/2 oz) butter

1 Butter 6 ramekin dishes and preheat the oven to 200°C/400°F/Gas 6.

2 Mash the crabmeat to a rough purée in a large bowl, then stir in the fromage frais. Add the Worcestershire sauce, mustard, sherry, cayenne pepper and salt and black pepper to taste.

3 Spoon the crab mixture into the prepared ramekins. Combine the breadcrumbs with the Parmesan cheese and sprinkle over the crab mixture. Dot with the butter and cook for 10 minutes until the topping is lightly browned.

NUTRITIONAL INFORMATION (PER SERVING)
Energy 1005 kJ/240 kcal ■ Protein 19 g ■ Carbohydrate 6 g ■ Fat 15 g

SPICY MUSHROOM BHAJIS

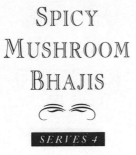

SERVES 4

THESE INDIAN-STYLE fritters make a delicious hot starter. For an interesting extra garnish, serve each portion with a spoonful of raita. Traditionally served as a cooling side dish for curry, raita is made by mixing natural yoghurt with chopped cucumber and mint. This recipe uses gram flour, made from ground chickpeas.

INGREDIENTS

150 g (5 oz) gram flour
1 egg, beaten
125 ml (4 1/2 fl oz) water
2.5 ml (1/2 tsp) ground turmeric
2.5 ml (1/2 tsp) ground coriander
2.5 ml (1/2 tsp) ground cumin
2.5 ml (1/2 tsp) chilli powder

salt and freshly ground black pepper
225 g (8 oz) button mushrooms, trimmed
vegetable oil, for frying
fresh coriander sprigs
lime slices, to garnish

1 Place the gram flour in a bowl. Make a well in the centre and add the egg and water. Using a wire whisk or an electric beater, gradually blend the flour into the liquid to make a smooth batter. Add the spices and salt and pepper to taste.

2 Heat the vegetable oil in a deep pan until hot. Dip a batch of mushrooms into the batter to coat evenly, then drop into the hot oil. Deep fry for about 3 minutes until golden. Remove with a slotted spoon, then drain on absorbent kitchen paper. Keep warm while frying the remaining mushrooms in batches. Serve hot, garnished with coriander sprigs and slices of lime.

NUTRITIONAL INFORMATION (PER SERVING)
Energy 880 kJ/210 kcal ■ *Protein 10 g* ■ *Carbohydrate 19 g* ■ *Fat 11 g*

THESE INDIVIDUAL MINI-quiches make a most attractive starter and, if there were any left over, would even go down well as part of a packed lunch on the following day! For delicious cocktail canapés, use a 12 bun tin and chop the peppers before adding to the filling or make some with bacon and mushroom.

STILTON AND PEPPER TARTLETS

SERVES 6

INGREDIENTS

75 g (3 oz) blue Stilton cheese without rind, crumbled
75 g (3 oz) curd cheese
200 ml (7 fl oz) milk
2 eggs, beaten

salt and freshly ground black pepper
$^1/_2$ green pepper, de-seeded and cut into 2.5 cm (1 in) sticks
$^1/_2$ red pepper, de-seeded and cut into 2.5 cm (1 in) sticks

PASTRY
225 g (8 oz) Glutafin Baking Mix
110 g (4 oz) margarine
30 ml (2 tbs) water

1 To make the pastry, put the Baking Mix and margarine in a mixing bowl and lightly rub together with your fingertips until the mixture resembles fine breadcrumbs. Add the water and cut in with a knife until the crumbs start to bind together. Bring together by hand to form a soft dough, leaving the bowl clean. Knead gently on a surface lightly floured with Mix and roll out between two sheets of greaseproof paper to the required size.

2 Preheat the oven to 200°C/400°F/Gas 6.

3 Using a saucer, cut the pastry into rounds and use to line 6 deep 10 cm (4 in) tartlet tins, trimming to fit. Mix the cheeses with the milk and eggs and season to taste with salt and pepper. Spoon into the pastry cases. Arrange green and red pepper sticks in a wheel pattern on each tartlet.

4 Bake the tartlets in the oven for 15 minutes until set. Serve hot or cold.

NUTRITIONAL INFORMATION (PER SERVING)
Energy 1515 kJ/362 kcal ▪ Protein 9 g ▪ Carbohydrate 34 g ▪ Fat 22 g

ASPARAGUS BUCKWHEAT PANCAKES

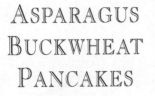

SERVES 4

THESE ASPARAGUS AND ham filled pancakes make an impressive start to a formal meal. For convenience, canned asparagus may be used instead of fresh asparagus.

Buckwheat grain is completely gluten-free. The flour has a distinctive rich flavour and is popular in Eastern Europe for making pancakes.

INGREDIENTS

50 g (2 oz) buckwheat flour
175 g (6 oz) Glutafin Baking Mix
2.5 ml (1/2 tsp) salt
1 egg, separated

350 ml (12 fl oz) milk
25 g (1 oz) margarine, melted
vegetable oil, for frying

ASPARAGUS FILLING

225 g (8 oz) fresh asparagus
150 g (5 oz) cottage cheese
150 ml (5 fl oz) smetana

1 egg, beaten
110 g (4 oz) cooked ham, chopped
freshly ground black pepper

1 Sift the flour, Baking Mix and salt into a bowl and stir in the egg yolk. Gradually add the milk and margarine, then beat well. Whisk the egg white until stiff and fold into the batter.

2 Heat a little oil in a small non-stick pan. Remove from the heat and pour off any excess oil. Pour in about 30 ml (2 tbs) batter, tilting the pan to spread the batter evenly. Cook over moderately high heat for 2 minutes until the top is beginning to look dry, then turn the pancake over. Cook the other side for 20-30 seconds until golden. Continue making pancakes, interleaving them with greaseproof paper.

3 To make the filling, steam the asparagus spears for 5 minutes and cut into 2.5 cm (1 in) pieces. Place in a bowl with the cottage cheese, 25 ml (1 fl oz) smetana, the beaten egg and chopped ham. Season to taste.

4 Preheat the oven to 180°C/350°F/Gas 4; grease a large ovenproof dish.

5 Place 2 tablespoons filling on each pancake and roll up. Arrange on the prepared dish, cover and bake for about 20 minutes until the pancakes are heated through. Serve with the remaining smetana poured on top.

NUTRITIONAL INFORMATION (PER SERVING)
Energy 2666 kJ/664 kcal ■ Protein 21 g ■ Carbohydrate 51 g ■ Fat 36 g

INDIVIDUAL BASIL-FLAVOURED salads are served with crisp bread sticks to make a refreshing Italian-style starter light enough to precede almost any main course. For a subtle variation, coat the bread sticks in poppy seeds instead of sesame seeds and try adding prawns to the salad. Dress with a vinaigrette to make a meal substantial enough to stand alone.

ITALIAN TOMATO SALAD WITH BREAD STICKS

SERVES 4

INGREDIENTS

SALAD

3 very large tomatoes

150 g (5 oz) Mozzarella cheese

1 large avocado

2 sprigs of fresh basil, roughly chopped

salt and freshly ground black pepper

20 black olives

45 ml (3 tbs) olive oil

BREAD STICKS

250 g (9 oz) Glutafin Baking Mix

110 ml (4 fl oz) tepid water

5 g (1/2 sachet) dried yeast

15 ml (1 tbs) vegetable oil

salt

1 egg, beaten

30-45 ml (2-3 tbs) sesame seeds

1 To make the bread sticks, first preheat the oven to 200°C-400°F/Gas 6. Combine the Baking Mix with the water, yeast, oil and salt to form a smooth, kneadable dough. Divide into 10 pieces and roll out into long stick shapes, brush with beaten egg and roll well in sesame seeds. Leave to stand for 20 minutes, then bake in the oven for 15- 20 minutes.

2 To make the salad, cut the tomatoes and cheese into 5mm (1/4 in) thick slices. Remove the stone and skin from the avocado and slice. Arrange the tomato, cheese and avocado in individual bowls or on plates, sprinkle over the basil and season to taste with salt and pepper. Scatter with olives.

3 Pour olive oil over each portion and serve at once with the bread sticks.

NUTRITIONAL INFORMATION (PER SERVING)
Tomato Salad: Energy 2320 kJ/554 kcal ■ Protein 9 g ■ Carbohydrate 54 g ■ Fat 35 g
Bread Sticks: Energy 1400 kJ/335 kcal ■ Protein 9 g ■ Carbohydrate 51 g ■ Fat 12 g

MAIN DISHES

THIS WHEAT-FREE version of a traditional favourite is sure to be a big hit. For individual pies use small pie dishes and bake for 25-30 minutes. Serve with potato and parsnip mash and steamed spring cabbage for a nourishing main course.

STEAK AND KIDNEY PIE

SERVES 6

INGREDIENTS

500 g (1 lb) chuck steak, cut into bite-sized pieces
110 g (4 oz) kidney, cut into bite-sized pieces
50 g (2 oz) mushrooms, sliced

1 small onion, chopped
15 ml (1 tbs) Glutafin Baking Mix
30 ml (2 tbs) beef stock
salt and freshly ground black pepper
beaten egg, to glaze

PASTRY
225 g (8 oz) Glutafin Baking Mix
110 g (4 oz) margarine
30 ml (2 tbs) water

1 Preheat the oven to 200°C/400°F/Gas 6.

2 To make the pastry, put the Baking Mix and margarine in a bowl and lightly rub together until the mixture resembles fine breadcrumbs. Add the water and cut in with a knife until the crumbs start to bind together. Bring together by hand to form a soft dough, then knead gently on a surface lightly floured with Baking Mix. Set one quarter of the pastry aside, and roll out the rest between two sheets of greaseproof paper. Use the rolled out pastry to line a 19 cm (7 1/2 in) round pie dish.

3 In a bowl, mix the chuck steak with the kidney, mushrooms, onion, Baking Mix and stock. Season to taste with salt and pepper, then spoon into the lined pie dish.

4 Roll out the reserved piece of pastry and use to cover the top of the pie. Seal the edges together by pressing the back of a fork around the pastry edge. Brush evenly with the beaten egg and cook in the oven for 20 minutes. Reduce the oven temperature to 170°C/325°F/Gas 3 and cook for 1 1/4 hours until the pie top is golden and the meat is cooked.

NUTRITIONAL INFORMATION (PER SERVING)
Energy 1876 kJ/448 kcal ▪ *Protein 31 g* ▪ *Carbohydrate 33 g* ▪ *Fat 22 g*

MARINATED ROAST BEEF WITH YORKSHIRE PUDDING

SERVES 8

GIVE SUNDAY LUNCH a new look with this delicious herb-flavoured roast beef dish, and serve with a revolutionary Yorkshire Pudding that is completely wheat-free.

Don't expect this old favourite to taste just like mother used to make, though – this is a version of Sunday lunch that is definitely not traditional!

INGREDIENTS

1.5 kg (3-3 1/2 lb) beef topside
45 ml (3 tbs) olive oil
150 ml (5 fl oz) red wine
5 ml (1 tsp) Dijon mustard
5 ml (1 tsp) dried thyme
1 bay leaf

salt and freshly ground black pepper
10 ml (2 tsp) cornflour
150 ml (5 fl oz) beef stock
5 ml (1 tsp) wheat-free creamed horseradish
oil, for greasing

YORKSHIRE PUDDING

3 eggs
110 g (4 oz) Rite-Diet Flour Mix

5 ml (1 tsp) gluten-free baking powder
200 ml (7 fl oz) soya milk

1 Place the beef in a shallow dish. In a separate bowl, combine the oil with the wine, mustard, thyme and bay leaf. Season to taste with salt and pepper, then pour over the meat. Cover and leave to marinate in a cool place for 8 hours, turning occasionally.

2 Meanwhile, prepare the Yorkshire pudding batter. Break the eggs into a bowl. Add the Flour Mix and baking powder and whisk with an electric mixer for a few minutes. Slowly add the soya milk, whisking continually. Leave to stand for 1 hour.

3 Pre-heat the oven to 200°C/400°F/Gas 6.

4 Transfer the beef to an oiled roasting tin, and reserve the marinade. Roast the beef for $1^1/4$-$1^1/2$ hours, turning halfway through cooking time, until the juices run slightly pink when the beef is tested with a skewer. Place the beef on a warmed serving dish and leave to stand. Drain off all but 30 ml (2 tbs) cooking juices from the tin.

5 Increase the oven temperature to 220°C/425°F/Gas 7. Oil an 18-hole bun tin and place in the oven for a few minutes to heat up. Pour a little batter into each bun indentation and bake in the oven for 15-20 minutes.

6 Meanwhile make the sauce. Strain the marinade into a measuring jug and make up to 300 ml (10 fl oz) with the stock. Blend the cornflour with the marinade and pour into the roasting tin. Bring to the boil, stirring well, then simmer for 1 minute or until thickened and smooth. Add the creamed horseradish and heat through. Season with salt and pepper to taste.

7 Carve the beef into slices and spoon over a little of the sauce. Serve the remaining sauce in a sauceboat.

NUTRITIONAL INFORMATION (PER SERVING)
Energy 2230 kJ/533 kcal ■ *Protein 54 g* ■ *Carbohydrate 13 g* ■ *Fat 27 g*

SWEET AND SOUR MEATBALLS

SERVES 6

SERVE WITH RICE noodles or rice and a steamed green vegetable for a tasty, well-balanced main course.

It is such an attractive dish it could be used for entertaining, but as a family standby, make it in large quantities and freeze. For a vegetarian version, use red lentils instead of the meat.

INGREDIENTS

225 g (8 oz) minced beef
225 g (8 oz) minced pork or veal
1 large onion, chopped
110 g (4 oz) fresh
wheat-free breadcrumbs
15 ml (1 tbs) finely chopped parsley
5 ml (1 tsp) dried mixed herbs

15 ml (1 tbs) Worcestershire sauce
15 ml (1 tbs) tomato purée
1 garlic clove, crushed
salt and freshly ground black pepper
2 eggs
25 ml (1 fl oz) vegetable oil

SWEET AND SOUR SAUCE

425 g (15 oz) can crushed pineapple
500 ml (17 fl oz) creamed tomatoes or
tomato juice
1 red pepper, de-seeded and chopped

5 ml (1 tsp) paprika
generous pinch of ground ginger
15 ml (1 tbs) wine vinegar

1 Preheat the oven to 180°C/350°F/Gas 4.

2 In a large bowl, mix the minced meat with the onion. Stir in the breadcrumbs, parsley, dried herbs, Worcestershire sauce, tomato purée and garlic. Season with salt and pepper, then add the beaten egg and mix thoroughly. Dust your hands with cornflour and roll the meat mixture into 18-20 balls.

3 Heat the oil in a large frying-pan, add the meatballs and fry, turning them frequently, until evenly browned. Drain on absorbent kitchen paper, then transfer to an ovenproof dish.

4 To make the sauce, combine the crushed pineapple with the creamed tomatoes, red pepper, paprika, ginger and wine vinegar. Season to taste.

5 Pour the sauce over the meatballs, cover the dish and bake in the oven for about 25 minutes until cooked through. Serve at once.

NUTRITIONAL INFORMATION (PER SERVING)
Energy 1275 kJ/305 kcal ■ Protein 19 g ■ Carbohydrate 25 g ■ Fat 15 g

CAPTURE THE FLAVOUR of the Mediterranean with these marinated lamb kebabs. Served with crunchy pine nut rice and a fresh green salad, they make a delightful meal for summer days — the combination of colours and textures is simply irresistible.

LAMB KEBABS WITH PINE NUT RICE

SERVES 4

INGREDIENTS

¹/2 leg of lamb, boned and cubed
1 red pepper, de-seeded
1 green pepper, de-seeded

1 onion, quartered
75 g (3 oz) button mushrooms
75 g (3 oz) cherry tomatoes

MARINADE
60 ml (4 tbs) olive oil
15 ml (1 tbs) wine vinegar
15 ml (1 tbs) lemon juice
15 ml (1 tbs) finely chopped mint
1 garlic clove, crushed

PINE NUT RICE
30 ml (2 tbs) olive oil
50 g (2 oz) pine nuts
225 g (8 oz) long-grain rice
400 ml (14 fl oz) chicken stock

1 Place the lamb in a bowl. Combine all the marinade ingredients and pour over the lamb. Leave to marinate in a cool place for about 4 hours.

2 To make the pine nut rice, heat the oil in a large pan, add the pine nuts and cook gently for about 5 minutes until golden. Add the rice and stir over moderate heat for 2-3 minutes until the grains are transparent. Pour in the chicken stock, bring to the boil, then reduce the heat slightly and simmer, covered, for about 15 minutes until the stock is absorbed and the rice is tender.

3 Meanwhile, prepare the kebabs. Heat the grill to medium high. Cut the peppers into squares, then thread the vegetables and meat alternately onto 8 skewers. Place on a rack in the grill pan, brush with the remaining marinade and grill, basting occasionally with the marinade, until the lamb is cooked through.

4 Serve the kebabs accompanied by the pine nut rice.

NUTRITIONAL INFORMATION (PER SERVING)
Energy 2876 kJ/684 kcal ▪ Protein 21 g ▪ Carbohydrate 51 g ▪ Fat 45 g

LAMB CUTLETS EN CROUTE

SERVES 4

WHEAT-FREE PASTRY parcels with a surprise meaty filling look impressive but are in fact, very easy to make. Serve with grilled tomatoes and mushrooms sautéed with chopped herbs for a special meal the whole family will enjoy.

A sprinkling of sesame seeds gives the pastry an extra dimension of flavour.

INGREDIENTS

8 lamb cutlets, trimmed
225 g (8 oz) Rite-Diet Flour Mix
110 g (4 oz) margarine
1 egg, lightly beaten
30-45 ml (2-3 tbs) water
beaten egg, to glaze
25 g (1 oz) sesame seeds, to decorate
30 ml (2 tbs) olive oil
15 ml (1 tbs) wine vinegar
1 garlic clove, crushed
10 ml (2 tsp) finely chopped mint

STUFFING
25 g (1 oz) margarine
1 onion, chopped
50 g (2 oz) long-grain rice, cooked
50 g (2 oz) dried apricots,
soaked and chopped
15 ml (1 tbs) seedless raisins
15 ml (1 tbs) pumpkin seeds
10 ml (2 tsp) finely grated lemon
rind
salt and freshly ground black pepper

1 Place the lamb in a shallow dish. Whisk together the oil, vinegar, garlic and mint, then pour over the meat. Leave to marinate for 30 minutes.

2 To make the stuffing, melt the margarine in a pan, add the onion and cook gently for 5 minutes until softened and lightly coloured. Stir in the rice, apricots, raisins, pumpkin seeds and lemon rind. Season with salt and pepper and set aside.

3 To make the pastry, put the Flour Mix and margarine in a mixing bowl and lightly rub together with your fingertips until the mixture resembles fine breadcrumbs. Add the egg and water and cut in with a knife until the crumbs start to bind together, then form into a soft dough by hand. Knead gently on a surface lightly floured with the Mix and roll out between two sheets of greaseproof paper into a square shape.

4 Preheat the oven to 220°C/425°F/Gas 7 and grease a baking sheet.

5 Using a sharp knife, cut the pastry into long strips about 2 cm (¾ in) wide. Place a tablespoon of stuffing on top of the 'eye' of each cutlet. Brush a strip of pastry with egg and wrap around one cutlet, overlapping the edges so that the lamb and stuffing are completely enclosed. Arrange the wrapped cutlets on the baking sheet and brush with egg to glaze.

6 Sprinkle the parcels with sesame seeds and bake in the oven for about 25-30 minutes until the pastry is golden brown.

NUTRITIONAL INFORMATION (PER SERVING)
Energy 3525 kJ/842 kcal ▪ *Protein 36 g* ▪ *Carbohydrate 66 g* ▪ *Fat 50 g*

LAMB AND THYME HOTPOT

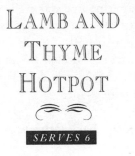

SERVES 6

A POTATO TOPPING makes an easy alternative to pastry — it is also very tasty. Here a layer of sliced potatoes tops a hearty lamb casserole to produce a nourishing all-in-one meal excellent on cold winter's evenings. As a variation, use puréed potatoes and pipe decoratively around the edge of the dish.

INGREDIENTS

1 kg (2 lb) boned shoulder of lamb, cut into 5 cm (2 in) cubes
25 g (1 oz) cornflour
salt and freshly ground black pepper
30 ml (2 tbs) vegetable oil
2 onions, chopped
225 g (8 oz) carrots, sliced
2 celery sticks, sliced

450 ml (15 fl oz) chicken stock
30 ml (2 tbs) tomato purée
5 ml (1 tsp) dried thyme
1 bay leaf
500 g (1 lb) potatoes
25 g (1 oz) margarine, melted
sprigs of thyme, to garnish

1 Preheat the oven to 190°C/375°F/Gas 5.

2 Toss the lamb cubes in the cornflour seasoned with salt and pepper. Shake off any excess cornflour and reserve.

3 Heat the oil in a frying-pan, add the lamb and brown on all sides. Remove from the pan with a slotted spoon and place in a large ovenproof casserole dish. Add the onions to the frying-pan and cook for 5 minutes until golden. Add the carrots and celery and cook for a few more minutes.

4 Stir the remaining cornflour into the vegetables. Add the stock, tomato purée and herbs and simmer, stirring continuously, until the sauce has thickened. Adjust the seasoning and transfer to the casserole. Combine well with the lamb.

5 Peel and evenly slice the potatoes, then arrange on top of the meat in overlapping layers. Brush with the melted margarine and cook in the oven for 1¹/4 - 1¹/2 hours until the meat is tender and the potato topping is browned. Garnish with thyme and serve.

NUTRITIONAL INFORMATION (PER SERVING)
Energy 2765 kJ/661 kcal ■ *Protein 27 g* ■ *Carbohydrate 25 g* ■ *Fat 51 g*

SERVE WITH AN interesting potato dish such as Duchesse potatoes - beat 50 g (2 oz) margarine and 1 large egg yolk into 1 kg (2 lb) mashed and sieved potato. Spoon into a large piping bag fitted with a star nozzle and pipe swirls onto a greased baking sheet. Brush with egg and brown in the oven.

SOMERSET PORK

SERVES 4

INGREDIENTS

25 g (1 oz) margarine
4 pork chops, trimmed
1 onion, chopped
2 celery sticks, sliced
2 carrots, sliced
25 g (1 oz) wheat-free flour
400 ml (15 fl oz) cider

60 ml (4 tbs) chicken stock
25 g (1 oz) seedless raisins
1 large cooking apple, diced or 8 dried apple slices
30 ml (2 tbs) tomato purée
1 bay leaf
salt and freshly ground black pepper

1 Preheat the oven to 200°C/400°F/Gas 6.

2 Melt the margarine in a large frying-pan and brown the chops on each side. Transfer to a casserole dish.

3 Add the onion, celery and carrots to the pan and fry for 3 minutes until the onion is beginning to soften. Stir in the flour, then gradually add the cider and stock, stirring continuously, and cook for a few minutes until thickened. Add the raisins, apple, tomato purée, bay leaf and salt and pepper to taste. Stir well and pour over the chops in the casserole dish.

4 Cover the dish and cook in the oven for about 45 minutes until the chops are cooked through.

NUTRITIONAL INFORMATION (PER SERVING)
Energy 1900 kJ/454 kcal ▪ Protein 17 g ▪ Carbohydrate 19 g ▪ Fat 35 g

CHICKEN KORMA

SERVES 6

ONE OF THE best-known Indian curries, a korma is made with yoghurt and spices – quite mild but wonderfully rich and spicy. It can also be made with lean pieces of lamb instead of chicken.

Serve with basmati rice for a traditional taste of the east.

INGREDIENTS

1.5 kg (3 lb) chicken	150 ml (5 fl oz) natural yoghurt
1 lemon, halved	45 ml (3 tbs) vegetable oil
salt and freshly ground black pepper	1 onion, sliced
1.5 ml (¼ tsp) chilli powder	1 garlic clove, crushed
5 ml (1 tsp) ground cumin	4 cardamom pods
5 ml (1 tsp) ground coriander	50 g (2 oz) creamed coconut
1.5 ml (¼ tsp) ground turmeric	150 ml (5 fl oz) warm water
2.5 ml (½ tsp) ground ginger	50 g (2 oz) unsalted cashew nuts
small cinnamon stick, crushed	fresh coriander sprigs, to garnish

1 Gently remove the skin from the chicken, starting at the front end, then cut into portions, wash and pat dry.

2 Place the chicken in a bowl large enough to hold the chicken in a single layer, then rub with the lemon, squeezing out the juice. Sprinkle with salt.

3 Mix the chilli powder, cumin, coriander, turmeric, ginger, cinnamon and a generous sprinkling of black pepper into the yoghurt and pour over the chicken pieces. Turn the chicken pieces to coat thoroughly, cover and leave to marinate for 2 hours.

4 Melt the oil in a large saucepan, add the onion and garlic and fry gently for 3 minutes until the onion is softened. Add the cardamom pods and cook for a further 1 minute.

5 Add the chicken to the pan, with the yoghurt marinade. Mix the creamed coconut with the water and stir into the pan. Cover and simmer for about 1 hour until the chicken is cooked. Stir in the cashew nuts and heat through for a few minutes.

6 Transfer to a warmed serving dish, garnish with coriander sprigs and serve at once.

NUTRITIONAL INFORMATION (PER SERVING)
Energy 1916 kJ/458 kcal ■ Protein 59 g ■ Carbohydrate 6 g ■ Fat 22 g

THIS EASY-TO-MAKE chicken dish is just the thing for a most nourishing family dinner.

Serve with jacket potatoes, which can be baked in the oven at the same time as the chicken to make a complete meal ideal for weekday evenings when time is short.

GOLDEN CHICKEN ✓

SERVES 6

INGREDIENTS

6 chicken quarters
50 g (2 oz) margarine
30 ml (2 tbs) Worcestershire sauce or gluten-free soy sauce

30 ml (2 tbs) clear honey
30 ml (2 tbs) lemon juice
salt and freshly ground black pepper

1 Preheat the oven to 180°C/350°F/Gas 4.

2 Wash the chicken pieces and pat dry with absorbent kitchen paper. Place skin-side down in an ovenproof dish.

3 Melt the margarine and stir in the Worcestershire sauce, honey and lemon juice. Season to taste with salt and pepper and pour over the chicken pieces. Cook uncovered in the oven for about 1 hour, turning once and basting regularly, until the chicken is cooked and has a golden glaze. Serve at once.

NUTRITIONAL INFORMATION (PER SERVING)
Energy 1790 kJ/428 kcal ■ *Protein 27 g* ■ *Carbohydrate 6 g* ■ *Fat 33 g*

VIENNESE TURKEY

SERVES 4

AS A FINISHING TOUCH, top each cooked escalope with a sprig of parsley and a wedge of lemon.

If wished, chicken breasts can be used instead of the turkey escalopes. To make dry breadcrumbs, see the recipe for Goujons of Sole, page 26.

INGREDIENTS

4 turkey breast escalopes, each weighing about 110 g (4 oz)
2 slices ham, halved
4 slices Gruyère cheese
wheat-free flour, for coating
salt and freshly ground black pepper

1 egg
200 g (7 oz) fine dry wheat-free breadcrumbs
45 ml (3 tbs) vegetable oil
fresh parsley sprigs and lemon wedges, to garnish

1 Horizontally slice each escalope through the centre, without cutting all the way through. Place half a slice of ham and one slice of cheese in the centre of each escalope.

2 Season the flour with salt and pepper. Break the egg into a bowl and beat well. Spread the breadcrumbs out on a plate. First coat the escalopes in the seasoned flour, then dip into the beaten egg and finally coat evenly with crumbs. Shake off any excess crumbs.

3 Heat the oil in a large frying-pan and cook 2 escalopes for 8-10 minutes until golden, turning once. Remove and drain on absorbent kitchen paper. Keep them warm while you cook the remaining escalopes. Serve hot, garnished with parsley sprigs and lemon wedges.

NUTRITIONAL INFORMATION (PER SERVING)
Energy 1700 kJ/406 kcal ▪ Protein 31 g ▪ Carbohydrate 20 g ▪ Fat 23 g

DELICATE SLICES OF grilled duck served with a red, fruity sauce make a delicious dinner party dish. Grilling the duck on a wire rack ensures that most of the fat runs away into the grill pan.

Accompanied by new potatoes and fine green beans, this simple yet stylish dish is sure to impress even would-be gourmêts with its fine combination of flavours and textures.

HONEY - GLAZED DUCK WITH RASPBERRY SAUCE

SERVES 4

INGREDIENTS

300 g (10 oz) raspberries
10 ml (2 tsp) caster sugar
4 boned duck breasts
1.5 ml ($^1/4$ tsp) ground coriander
salt and freshly ground black pepper

15 ml (1 tbs) vegetable oil
25 g (1 oz) margarine or butter
30 ml (2 tbs) clear honey
60 ml (4 tbs) wine
fresh coriander sprigs, to serve

1 Purée the raspberries by pressing through a sieve, then sweeten with caster sugar. Set aside.

2 Score the skin of the duck breasts in a criss-cross pattern with a sharp knife, then season with coriander and salt and pepper.

3 Heat the grill to medium high.

4 Arrange the duck, skin-side up, on the wire rack of the grill pan (so that the fat can fall away). Grill the duck for about 10 minutes on each side, then brush with honey. Transfer to an oven roasting dish and bake in a preheated moderate oven for a further 20 minutes.

5 Drain off the excess fat from the pan juices, stir in the wine and boil rapidly for 1 minute, stirring well and scraping up the sediment from the base of the pan. Remove from the heat stir in the raspberry purée. Gently heat through.

6 Slice the duck and arrange on individual plates, surrounded by the sauce. Garnish with coriander and serve.

NUTRITIONAL INFORMATION (PER SERVING)
Energy 3905 kJ/933 kcal ■ *Protein 22 g* ■ *Carbohydrate 14 g* ■ *Fat 87 g*

TUNA AND SPINACH LASAGNE

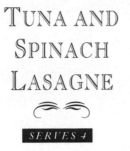

SERVES 4

THIS DELICIOUS LASAGNE is ideal for an informal gathering or family meal. If wished, a traditional minced beef and tomato sauce can be used with great success.

The method for making pasta can, of course, be used for all the other varieties if you enjoy making fresh pasta.

INGREDIENTS

225 g (8 oz) fresh spinach
25 g (1 oz) margarine
1 small onion, chopped
25 g (1 oz) cornflour
300 ml (10 fl oz) milk

200 g (7 oz) can tuna fish, drained
50 g (2 oz) button mushrooms, sliced
salt and freshly ground black pepper
50 g (2 oz) Cheddar cheese, grated
2.5 ml (1/2 tsp) grated nutmeg

HOME-MADE PASTA

150 g (5 oz) Rite-Diet Flour Mix
2 eggs
15 ml (1 tbs) vegetable oil

1 To make the pasta, place the Flour Mix in a bowl. Make a well in the centre, add the eggs and oil to the well and gradually work in the flour to form a dough. Knead the dough with your hands for 5-8 minutes until it becomes smooth and elastic. Divide into 4 equal pieces. Roll dough 2-3 times through the widest setting on a pasta machine, folding in half and turning each time, or rest the dough, covered, for 15-30 minutes and roll out by hand as above. When the dough is smooth, run it unfolded through the rollers until you reach number 4 setting, or roll out by hand until the required thickness is achieved.

2 Cook the lasagne sheets in boiling water, with a little oil and salt added, for about 5 minutes until *al dente*. Drain.

3 Remove the stalks from the spinach and wash well. Place in a saucepan with no extra water and cook over a moderate heat for about 10 minutes. Drain and chop.

4 Preheat the oven to 180°C/350°F/Gas 4 and grease a large ovenproof dish.

5 To make the tuna sauce, melt the margarine, add the onion and cook for about 3 minutes until softened. Add the cornflour and cook for 1 minute, stirring. Remove from the heat and gradually stir in the milk. Return to the heat and cook, stirring continuously, until the sauce is thickened and smooth. Gently stir the tuna and mushrooms into the sauce and season to taste with salt and pepper.

6 To assemble the lasagne, spread a layer of tuna sauce over the base of the dish, followed by a layer of chopped spinach and a sprinkling of nutmeg, followed by a layer of pasta. Repeat these three layers, finishing with a layer of tuna sauce. Sprinkle over the cheese.

7 Bake the lasagne for 25-30 minutes until the cheese is bubbling. Serve at once.

NUTRITIONAL INFORMATION (PER SERVING)
Energy 1805 kJ/432 kcal ■ *Protein 22 g* ■ *Carbohydrate 27 g* ■ *Fat 27 g*

HERB - STUFFED PLAICE IN WINE

SERVES 4

PLAICE FILLETS ROLLED up with a herby filling and bathed in a creamy wine sauce look sophisticated and taste divine. Surprisingly easy to make, this dish would make an excellent main course for a dinner party. Serve with mange tout and carrot sticks.

If wished, the single cream can be replaced with Greek yoghurt or fromage frais for a lower-fat version which is no less tasty.

INGREDIENTS

4 large plaice fillets
25 g (1 oz) margarine or butter
1 small onion, grated
75 g (3 oz) fresh wheat-free
breadcrumbs
finely grated rind of 1 lemon
15 ml (1 tbs) finely chopped parsley
30 ml (2 tbs) finely chopped dill

1 large egg, beaten
50 g (2 oz) button mushrooms,
finely chopped
salt and freshly ground black pepper
150 ml (5 fl oz) dry white wine
60 ml (4 tbs) single cream
fresh dill sprigs, to garnish

1 Skin the plaice fillets and halve lengthways. Rinse and pat dry with absorbent kitchen paper. Preheat the oven to 180°C/350°F/Gas 4.

2 Melt the margarine in a pan, add the onion and cook gently for 5 minutes until softened. In a bowl, mix the breadcrumbs with the lemon rind, parsley and the dill. Add the fried onion, egg and half the mushrooms and stir well. Season to taste with salt and pepper.

3 Spread the filling on the skinned side of each fillet and roll up from the tail end. Arrange in a shallow ovenproof dish, join-side down, and pour the wine into the dish with the remaining mushrooms. Cover and poach for about 20 minutes until cooked.

4 Using a slotted spoon, transfer the cooked plaice rolls to a warmed serving dish. Boil the remaining wine briskly for 2 minutes to reduce, add the cream, and heat through gently. Adjust the seasoning and pour the sauce over the plaice rolls. Garnish with dill sprigs and serve at once.

NUTRITIONAL INFORMATION (PER SERVING)
Energy 1045 kJ/250 kcal ■ Protein 26 g ■ Carbohydrate 10 g ■ Fat 12 g

IDEAL FOR A SUMMER lunch or light evening meal, this elegant quiche is delicious hot or cold when served with a tossed mixed salad.

If wished, ham and mushrooms can be substituted for the salmon and red pepper to ring the changes.

SALMON QUICHE

SERVES 6

INGREDIENTS

75 g (3 oz) cottage cheese
2 spring onions, chopped
1/2 red pepper, de-seeded and chopped
salt and freshly ground black pepper

120 g (4 oz) can red or pink salmon
2 eggs
200 ml (7 fl oz) milk
fresh parsley sprigs, to garnish

PASTRY

200 g (7 oz) Glutafin Baking Mix
25 g (1 oz) wheat-free fibre or bran
75 g (3 oz) margarine
45 ml (3 tbs) water

1 Preheat the oven to 200°C/400°F/Gas 6.

2 To make the pastry, put the Baking Mix, fibre and margarine in a mixing bowl and lightly rub together with your fingertips until the mixture resembles fine breadcrumbs. Add the water and cut in with a knife until the crumbs start to bind together. Bring together by hand to form a soft dough. Knead gently on a surface lightly floured with Baking Mix and roll out between two sheets of greaseproof paper. Use to line a 20 cm (8 in) flan ring.

3 Combine the cheese, onions and red pepper, season with salt and pepper, then spoon into the flan case. Drain and flake the salmon and spread over the cheese mixture. Beat the eggs with the milk and pour into the pastry case.

4 Bake in the oven for about 30 minutes until the filling is turning golden. Serve hot or cold garnished with parsley sprigs.

NUTRITIONAL INFORMATION (PER SERVING)
Energy 1275 kJ/305 kcal ■ Protein 12 g ■ Carbohydrate 30 g ■ Fat 16 g

VERMOUTH TROUT IN FOIL

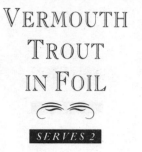

SERVES 2

TROUT BAKED WITH vermouth and fennel is a simple yet exquisite dish you will want to serve again and again.

Cooking the trout in foil keeps it moist, enhancing the delicate flavour and texture of the fish. Serve with baked tomatoes and new potatoes for a truly palate-tingling meal.

INGREDIENTS

2 trout, cleaned
1/2 fennel bulb
25 g (1 oz) butter

salt and freshly ground black pepper
15 ml (1 tbs) finely chopped parsley
30 ml (2 tbs) dry vermouth

1 Preheat the oven to 170°C/325°F/Gas 3.

2 Chop the fennel, reserving the feathery leaves for garnishing.

3 Grease 2 pieces of double-thickness kitchen foil with butter and place a trout in the centre of each. Season the fish generously with salt and pepper, then dot with the remaining butter. Sprinkle with the parsley and arrange the chopped fennel around the trout. Spoon 15 ml (1 tbs) vermouth over each fish.

4 Fold over the edges of the foil to make loose but airtight parcels and bake in the oven for 30 minutes until the fish is cooked.

5 To serve, unwrap the foil and carefully transfer the fish, with the fennel and juices, to individual heated plates. Garnish with the reserved fennel leaves.

NUTRITIONAL INFORMATION (PER SERVING)
Energy 985 kJ/235 kcal ■ Protein 24 g ■ Carbohydrate 1 g ■ Fat 15 g

SPAIN'S MOST FAMOUS dish, Paella is a meal in itself. This version uses chicken, bacon, mussels and prawns, but you can vary the meat and fish ingredients as you like. For speed, use canned mussels instead of fresh.

PAELLA

SERVES 8

INGREDIENTS

12 unshelled mussels
1 kg (2 lb) chicken, cut into 8 pieces
salt and freshly ground black pepper
50 ml (2 fl oz) olive oil
6 rashers lean bacon, chopped
1 onion, chopped
2 garlic cloves, crushed
1 red pepper, de-seeded and sliced
4 tomatoes, skinned and chopped

5 ml (1 tsp) paprika
400 g (14 oz) long-grain rice
1 L (1 3/4 pt) chicken stock
a generous pinch of saffron powder or ground turmeric
110 g (4 oz) peeled prawns
1 can artichoke hearts, drained
110 g (4 oz) frozen petit pois, defrosted

1 Check that the unshelled mussels are fresh by tapping any open ones against the chopping board - discard any that do not shut. Scrub clean. Soak in cold water for 2-3 hours, changing the water several times, then drain. Cook the mussels in about 150 ml (5 fl oz) boiling water in a large pan until they open. Discard any unopened ones and set the rest aside.

2 Season the chicken with salt and pepper. Heat half the oil in a large frying-pan, add the chicken and bacon and fry for about 10-15 minutes, turning frequently, until the chicken is golden on all sides. Remove the chicken and bacon from the pan and set aside.

3 Heat remaining oil in the pan. Add the onion, garlic, red pepper and tomatoes and cook gently for 5 minutes until onion is soft. Stir in the paprika and rice and cook for 1 minute, stirring. Remove from heat.

4 Bring the stock to the boil and stir in the saffron. Pour the stock into the frying-pan and stir well. Bring to the boil and cook for 5 minutes. Arrange the chicken, bacon, mussels, peeled prawns and artichoke hearts on top of the rice. Sprinkle over the peas. Cook over low heat for about 20 minutes until the rice is tender and the liquid absorbed. Turn off the heat, cover the pan and leave to stand for 5 minutes. Serve.

NUTRITIONAL INFORMATION (PER SERVING)
Energy 1950 kJ/466 kcal ▪ *Protein 41 g* ▪ *Carbohydrate 47 g* ▪ *Fat 14 g*

SOYA AND NUT LOAF

SERVES 4

SERVED WITH A wine-flavoured tomato sauce, this tasty loaf makes an interesting vegetarian main course.

To skin the tomatoes, make a small cut in each tomato, then cover with boiling water for 1 minute. Drain and peel off the thin skin.

INGREDIENTS

150 g (5 oz) soya beans, soaked
15 ml (1 tbs) vegetable oil
150 g (5 oz) onions, chopped
110 g (4 oz) mushrooms, sliced
150 g (5 oz) hazelnuts or
brazil nuts, ground
75 g (3 oz) fresh wheat-free

breadcrumbs
25 g (1 oz) soya bran flakes
15 ml (1 tbs) finely chopped thyme
30 ml (2 tbs) tomato purée
10 ml (2 tsp) Worcestershire sauce
1 egg, beaten
salt and freshly ground black pepper

FRESH TOMATO SAUCE

15 ml (1 tbs) olive oil
1 onion, chopped
750 g (1 1/2 lbs) tomatoes,
skinned and chopped
15 ml (1 tbs) tomato purée

5 ml (1 tsp) sugar
45 ml (3 tbs) red wine
15 ml (1 tbs) chopped celery leaf
salt and freshly ground black pepper

1 Preheat the oven to 180°C/350°F/Gas 4 and grease a 500 ml (1 lb) loaf tin.

2 Parboil the soaked soya beans for 10 minutes. Drain and reserve.

3 Heat the oil in a saucepan, add the chopped onions and cook for 3 minutes until soft. Add the mushrooms and cook for a further 3 minutes. Add the soya beans, nuts, breadcrumbs, soya bran flakes, thyme, tomato purée and Worcestershire sauce. Bind together with the beaten egg and season with salt and pepper.

4 Press the soya mixture into the prepared loaf tin. Cover with kitchen foil and bake for about 1 hour until set.

5 Meanwhile, make the tomato sauce. Heat the oil, add the onion and cook until softened. Add the tomatoes, tomato purée, sugar, wine and celery leaf and season to taste with salt and pepper. Cover and simmer gently for about 30 minutes until the tomatoes are very mushy. Cool for about 10 minutes, then transfer to a food processor or blender and work until smooth. Press through a sieve to remove the pips. Reheat gently and adjust the seasoning.

6 Turn the cooked soya loaf out onto a serving dish and serve with the tomato sauce handed separately in a jug.

NUTRITIONAL INFORMATION (PER SERVING)
Energy 2070 kJ/495 kcal ▪ *Protein 17 g* ▪ *Carbohydrate 25 g* ▪ *Fat 37 g*

VEGETABLE COBBLER

SERVES 6

FOR A SATISFYING main dish that is packed with goodness, this wholesome vegetable cobbler is hard to beat. The herby scone topping is also excellent with a minced meat base — try it with extra-lean beef or lamb on cold winter's evenings.

INGREDIENTS

225 g (8 oz) haricot beans, soaked
30 ml (2 tbs) vegetable oil
1 garlic clove, crushed
1 aubergine, cubed
2 courgettes, sliced
2 leeks, sliced

1 green pepper, de-seeded and sliced
400 g (14 oz) can chopped tomatoes
600 ml (1 pt) vegetable stock
15 ml (1 tbs) tomato purée
salt and freshly ground black pepper

SCONE TOPPING

225 g (8 oz) Glutafin Baking Mix
1.5 ml (1/4 tsp) salt
50 g (2 oz) margarine
1/2 onion, finely chopped

1.5 ml (1/4 tsp) dried mixed herbs
75 ml (3 fl oz) milk
milk, to glaze

1 Boil the soaked haricot beans in a saucepan for 1 hour. Drain.

2 Heat the oil in a saucepan and add the garlic, aubergine, courgettes, leeks and green pepper. Cook gently for a few minutes until slightly golden. Add the tomatoes, stock, tomato purée, cooked beans and salt and pepper to taste. Cover and simmer for about 30 minutes, stirring occasionally. Transfer to a casserole dish.

3 Preheat the oven to 200°C/400°F/Gas 6.

4 To make the scone topping, put the Baking Mix and salt in a mixing bowl. Rub in the margarine until the mixture resembles breadcrumbs. Stir in the chopped onion and herbs, then add the milk and bring together to form a soft dough. Knead lightly until smooth. Roll or pat out to about 1 cm (1/2 in) thick and cut into 5 cm (2 in) rounds.

5 Place overlapping circles of the scone rounds on top of the vegetables in the casserole. Brush with a little milk and bake in the oven for about 30 minutes until the topping is golden brown. Serve at once.

NUTRITIONAL INFORMATION (PER SERVING)
Energy 1653 kJ/349 kcal ■ Protein 8 g ■ Carbohydrate 44 g ■ Fat 33 g

SIMPLE SUPPERS

BAKED STUFFED PEPPERS

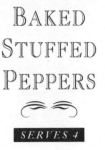

SERVES 4

THESE RICE-STUFFED peppers make a substantial all-in-one supper. Use vegetables as they come into season — try courgettes, aubergines and tomatoes — and bear in mind they could also be used as a side dish to accompany meat, or as a starter. Try cooking them in the microwave for a really quick meal.

INGREDIENTS

4 large red peppers
15 ml (1 tbs) vegetable oil
1 onion, chopped
1 garlic clove, crushed
110 g (4 oz) brown rice
50 g (2 oz) mushrooms, sliced

2 tomatoes, skinned and chopped
15 ml (1 tbs) tomato purée
5 ml (1 tsp) dried thyme or marjoram
salt and freshly ground black pepper
75 g (3 oz) Cheddar cheese, grated

1 Preheat the oven to 170°C/325°F/Gas 3.

2 Slice the tops off the peppers, then cut in half lengthways and de-seed. Place in a large ovenproof dish.

3 Heat the oil in a pan, add the onion and garlic and fry gently for about 3 minutes until softened. Add the rice and enough water to just cover the rice. Cook over gentle heat for about 15 minutes. Add the mushrooms, tomatoes, tomato purée, thyme and salt and pepper to taste.

4 Divide the mixture between the pepper halves and cover with kitchen foil. Bake in the oven for 30 minutes until the pepper is soft. Remove the foil and sprinkle with cheese. Return to the oven for a further 10 minutes until the cheese is bubbling and golden brown. Serve at once.

NUTRITIONAL INFORMATION (PER SERVING)
Energy 1682 kJ/280 kcal ■ Protein 9 g ■ Carbohydrate 30 g ■ Fat 15 g

THE BASE FOR this pizza does not need to be left to rise making it ideal for an instant family meal. The topping can be varied according to personal preference – mushrooms, peppers or sardines make excellent additions or try using whatever you have left in the store cupboard or refrigerator.

QUICK AND EASY PIZZA

SERVES 2

INGREDIENTS

275 g (10 oz) Glutafin Baking Mix
generous pinch of salt

1 egg
150 ml (5 fl oz) natural yoghurt

TOPPING

15 g (¹/2 oz) margarine
1 onion, chopped
200 g (7 oz) can tomatoes
15 ml (1 tbs) tomato purée
1.5 ml (¹/4 tsp) dried oregano
or marjoram

freshly ground black pepper
25 g (1 oz) anchovy fillets, drained
110 g (4 oz) Mozzarella or
Cheddar cheese, grated
6 black olives, stoned

1 Preheat the oven to 200°C/400°F/Gas 6.

2 Place the Baking Mix and salt in a mixing bowl. Beat the egg with the yoghurt and gradually mix into the dry ingredients until a soft dough is formed. Knead lightly on a surface lightly floured with Baking Mix and roll out to a round large enough to cover the base of a 20 cm (8 in) round baking tin or dish.

3 To make the topping, melt the margarine in a pan, add the onion and cook gently for 3 minutes until softened. Add the canned tomatoes and purée. Stir in the herbs and season to taste with salt and pepper. Simmer, stirring, until reduced to a rich sauce.

4 Spread the topping over the pizza base and arrange the anchovy fillets on top. Cover with the grated cheese and top with the black olives. Bake in the oven for about 25 minutes until the base is cooked through and the cheese is beginning to brown.

NUTRITIONAL INFORMATION (PER SERVING)
Energy 3265 kJ/780 kcal ■ *Protein 31 g* ■ *Carbohydrate 122 g* ■ *Fat 22 g*

CHICKEN STIR - FRY

SERVES 4

THERE IS NO more versatile dish than a stir-fry. Vary the ingredients as you wish - try prawns instead of chicken, or leave out the meat or fish altogether and add more vegetables and nuts for a vegetarian version. Frying in sesame oil imparts a flavour at once delicious and distinctive.

INGREDIENTS

10 ml (2 tsp) cornflour
30 ml (2 tbs) tamari or gluten-free soy sauce
10 ml (2 tsp) dry sherry
5 ml (1 tsp) sugar
150 ml (5 fl oz) water
30 ml (2 tbs) sesame or corn oil
225 g (8 oz) boned chicken breast, sliced

4 spring onions, sliced
1 garlic clove, crushed
1/2 red or green pepper, de-seeded and sliced
110 g (4 oz) mushrooms, sliced
110 g (4 oz) baby sweetcorn
110 g (4 oz) mange tout
50 g (2 oz) cashew nuts
110 g (4 oz) fresh beansprouts

1 In a bowl, blend the cornflour with the tamari sauce, sherry, sugar and water. Set aside.

2 Heat half the oil in a large frying-pan or wok, add the chicken and fry over fairly high heat, stirring, for about 5 minutes until cooked through. Remove from the pan with a slotted spoon and add the remaining oil.

3 Add the spring onions, garlic and pepper and fry, stirring, for 3 minutes. Stir in the mushrooms, sweetcorn and mange tout and continue to fry for 2 minutes. Add the blended cornflour mixture, together with the cooked chicken, cashew nuts and beansprouts. Toss together and simmer for 2-3 minutes until the beansprouts begin to soften.

4 Serve at once with cooked rice noodles or brown rice.

NUTRITIONAL INFORMATION (PER SERVING)
Energy 1690 kJ/404 kcal ■ Protein 19 g ■ Carbohydrate 49 g ■ Fat 16 g

CHICKEN LIVERS ARE extremely nutritious, but some people just can't bear offal in any shape or form. If that is the case, simply substitute small pieces of chicken breast for the livers. This is an inexpensive dish that can be cooked in one pan on a gas ring or hob – ideal for students on a tight budget.

CHICKEN LIVER RISOTTO

SERVES 6

INGREDIENTS

45 ml (3 tbs) vegetable oil
1 garlic clove, crushed
225 g (8 oz) chicken livers, chopped
110 g (4 oz) mushrooms, sliced
1 onion, chopped
150 g (5 oz) long-grain rice
600 ml (1 pt) chicken stock
45 ml (3 tbs) dry white wine
or sherry

salt and freshly ground black pepper
25 g (1 oz) currants
110 g (4 oz) can peas and carrots,
drained
25 g (1 oz) toasted almonds
or pine nuts
1 yellow pepper, diced
chopped parsley, to garnish

1 Heat the oil in a heavy-based saucepan, add the garlic and chicken livers and fry for 2-3 minutes. Remove from the pan and set aside. Add the mushrooms to the pan and fry gently for 3 minutes, then remove from the pan and set aside.

2 Add the onion to the pan and cook gently for about 5 minutes until soft and golden. Add the rice and continue to cook, stirring continuously, until the rice turns transparent. Pour in the stock and wine, then season to taste with salt and pepper. Cover tightly and cook over a moderate heat for about 15 minutes until the liquid has been absorbed.

3 Stir in the currants, nuts and the cooked chicken livers and mushrooms, peas, carrots and yellow pepper. Remove from the heat and leave to stand, still covered, for 10 minutes. Sprinkle with chopped parsley to garnish.

NUTRITIONAL INFORMATION (PER SERVING)
Energy 1871 kJ/446 kcal ■ *Protein 18 g* ■ *Carbohydrate 45 g* ■ *Fat 21 g*

CELEBRATION CHICKEN SALAD

SERVES 4

THIS IS A VERY tasty way of using up leftover chicken or turkey. If you wish you could use cooked long-grain rice instead of the pasta.

Made in large quantities, Celebration Chicken is an ideal buffet-table dish. As its name suggests, it is meant to be served at parties!

INGREDIENTS

150 g (5 oz) gluten-free
pasta spirals
salt and freshly ground black pepper
110 ml (4 fl oz) mayonnaise
45 ml (3 tbs) Greek yoghurt
15 ml (1 tbs) curry powder
5 ml (1 tsp) chutney
10 ml (2 tsp) tomato sauce

5 ml (1 tsp) lemon juice
60 ml (4 tbs) water
175 g (6 oz) cooked chicken
4 spring onions, chopped
2 celery sticks, chopped
1 red eating apple, chopped
snipped mustard and cress, to garnish

1 Cook the pasta in boiling salted water for 5-7 minutes until *al dente*. Drain, then rinse under cold running water and drain again.

2 In a bowl, mix the mayonnaise and yoghurt together. Add the curry powder, chutney, tomato sauce, lemon juice and water and stir well.

3 Cut the chicken into bite-sized pieces and stir into the sauce. Add the cooked pasta, spring onions, celery and apple. Mix well and season to taste with salt and pepper. Chill until you are ready to serve.

4 Arrange on a bed of lettuce, garnish with snipped mustard and cress and serve.

NUTRITIONAL INFORMATION (PER SERVING)
Energy 1730 kJ/413 kcal ■ Protein 17 g ■ Carbohydrate 32 g ■ Fat 25 g

THIS DELICIOUS PASTA dish is so quick and easy it makes an excellent 'standby' for weekday suppers. It is also a good way of using up leftover vegetables, as the ingredients in the sauce can be varied slightly to suit what is in your fridge. Serve with a mixed salad and perhaps a glass or two of Chianti!

PASTA ALLA CARBONARA

SERVES 4

INGREDIENTS

225 g (8 oz) wheat-free macaroni
salt and freshly ground black pepper
225 g (8 oz) rindless lean
bacon, chopped
1 onion, chopped
225 g (8 oz) mushrooms, sliced

1 garlic clove, crushed (optional)
2 large eggs
60 ml (4 tbs) single cream
finely grated Parmesan cheese,
to serve

1 Cook the macaroni in boiling salted water for about 10 minutes until *al dente*. Drain.

2 Fry the bacon and onion together in a pan for 4 minutes until the bacon is lightly browned. Add the mushrooms and garlic, if using, and fry gently for 5 minutes until the mushrooms are cooked.

3 Whisk the eggs and cream together and stir into the bacon mixture away from the heat. Pour the sauce over the cooked pasta, sprinkle with Parmesan cheese and serve at once.

NUTRITIONAL INFORMATION (PER SERVING)
Energy 1575 kJ/376 kcal ■ *Protein 22 g* ■ *Carbohydrate 48g* ■ *Fat 12 g*

CHILLI TACOS

SERVES 6

THIS MEXICAN-STYLE supper dish uses ready-made taco shells which are now available from larger supermarkets. Made from traditional Mexican tortillas (eggless cornmeal pancakes) taco shells are very handy for quick and easy wheat-free meals.

INGREDIENTS

15 ml (1 tbs) corn oil
1 onion, chopped
1 garlic clove, crushed
1 green pepper, de-seeded and chopped
375 g (12 oz) minced beef
25 g (1 oz) rice or potato flour
300 ml (10 fl oz) stock
60 ml (4 tbs) tomato purée

1.5-2.5 ml (^{1}/4-^{1}/2 tsp) chilli powder
5 ml (1 tsp) ground cumin
5 ml (1 tsp) dried oregano
225 g (8 oz) can red kidney beans, drained
salt and freshly ground black pepper
12 taco shells

60 ml (4 tbs) soured cream or yoghurt (optional)
1 avocado, sliced, to garnish

1 Heat the oil in a frying-pan, add the onion, garlic and pepper and cook gently for 5 minutes until the onion is soft and lightly coloured. Add the beef and cook briskly for 3 minutes to brown. Drain off the fat. Stir in the flour to absorb any remaining fat, then add the stock, tomato purée, chilli powder, cumin, oregano, kidney beans and salt and pepper to taste. Bring to the boil, then lower the heat and simmer for 30 minutes.

2 Preheat the oven to 180°C/350°F/Gas 4.

3 About 5 minutes before serving, heat the taco shells in the oven until crisp. Spoon the beef mixture into the taco shells and top with a little soured cream, if using. Peel, stone and slice the avocado and arrange in the tacos. Serve at once.

NUTRITIONAL INFORMATION (PER SERVING)
Energy 1340 kJ/320 kcal ■ Protein 22 g ■ Carbohydrate 21 g ■ Fat 17 g

CHILDREN WILL LOVE these nutritious fish-shaped patties. For the best way to make dry breadcrumbs, see the recipe for Goujons of Sole, page 26. As you are bound to be asked for these again and again, why not make them in large amounts and freeze?

FUN
FISH CAKES

SERVES 6

INGREDIENTS

250 g (9 oz) cod or haddock
fillet, skinned
250 g (9 oz) potatoes
15 g (¹/2 oz) margarine
30 ml (2 tbs) milk
1 egg, hard-boiled
10 ml (2 tsp) finely chopped parsley

salt and freshly ground black pepper
1 egg, beaten for coating
110 g (4 oz) fine dry wheat-free
breadcrumbs
vegetable oil, for frying
3 stuffed green olives, halved
lemon wedges, to garnish

1 Put the fish in a saucepan and cover with a little cold water. Bring to the boil, then lower the heat and simmer very gently for about 10 minutes. Remove the fish with a slotted spoon and cool. Meanwhile, boil the potatoes in salted water for about 15 minutes until soft, then drain and mash. Beat in the margarine and milk.

2 Flake the fish and stir into the mashed potato. Finely chop the hard-boiled egg and add to the fish mixture with the parsley. Season to taste with salt and pepper. Divide into 6 portions and form into fish shapes.

3 Spread the breadcrumbs out on a flat plate. Brush the cakes with beaten egg, then press in the breadcrumbs until thoroughly and evenly coated. Shallow fry the fish cakes in oil for about 5 minutes on each side, until golden brown. Drain on absorbent kitchen paper.

4 To serve, position an olive slice on each fish cake to represent eyes and garnish with lemon wedges.

NUTRITIONAL INFORMATION (PER SERVING)
Energy 780 kJ/187 kcal ▪ *Protein 11 g* ▪ *Carbohydrate 14 g* ▪ *Fat 10 g*

CAPTIONS FOR
THE FOLLOWING
FIVE COLOUR PAGES

Page 1 *(opposite)*
Classic Minestrone Soup *(page 16)*

Page 2 *(overleaf)*
TOP Italian Tomato Salad
with Bread Sticks *(page 31)*
BOTTOM Salmon Cheese Puffs *(page 25)*

Page 3
Asparagus Buckwheat Pancakes *(page 30)*

Page 4-5
FROM LEFT TO RIGHT
Tuna and Spinach Lasagne *(page 48)*
Paella *(page 51)*
Sweet and Sour Meatballs *(page 36)*

CAPTIONS FOR
THE PRECEDING
THREE COLOUR PAGES

❧ ❧

Page 6
Steak and Kidney Pie *(page 33)*

❧ ❧

Page 7
Herb-stuffed Plaice in Wine *(page 46)*

❧ ❧

Page 8 *(opposite)*
TOP Chef's Salad *(page 69)*
BOTTOM Mushroom and
Spinach Roulade *(page 66)*

CRISPY HERRINGS WITH MUSTARD SAUCE

SERVES 2

A TASTY VARIATION of a classic Scottish dish, herrings coated in buckwheat flakes make a nutritious simple supper served with baked potatoes and a green vegetable. Herrings are rich in vitamins A and D which are vital for good health, so it makes sense to include this type of fish in your diet.

Fried or grilled herrings also marry well with a fresh-tasting gooseberry sauce.

INGREDIENTS

1 fresh herring
salt and freshly ground black pepper
15 g (1/2 oz) Rite-Diet Hot
Breakfast Cereal or buckwheat flakes
30 ml (2 tbs) vegetable oil,
for frying

MUSTARD SAUCE
20 g (3/4 oz) margarine
20 g (3/4 oz) cornflour
150 ml (5 fl oz) milk
10 ml (2 tsp) French mustard

1 To fillet the herring, lay the fish on its side and cut around the head, following the bone structure, then slice along the backbone from the head to the tail. Lift the top flesh at the sliced opening, insert the knife and cut the top fillet away from the backbone, taking care to avoid the rib bones. Turn the fish over and cut out the other fillet in the same way. Trim the fillets and season with salt and pepper.

2 Roll the fillets in the cereal to coat evenly. Heat the oil in a frying-pan, add the coated fillets and cook for about 5 minutes on each side until golden and cooked through.

3 Meanwhile, make the sauce. Combine the margarine, cornflour, milk and mustard in a small pan. Bring to the boil over gentle heat, stirring continuously, and simmer for a few minutes until thickened. Season to taste with salt and pepper.

4 Transfer the cooked fish to a warmed serving dish and pour over the mustard sauce.

NUTRITIONAL INFORMATION (PER SERVING)
Energy 1730 kJ/414 kcal ■ Protein 10 g ■ Carbohydrate 18 g ■ Fat 34 g

IN THIS UNUSUAL vegetarian meal, aubergines are used to line the baking dish in the same way that bread is used in a charlotte. Filled with layers of tomato sauce, yoghurt and breadcrumbs, it makes a substantial supper dish and is sure to be equally popular with habitual meat-eaters — a low-fat alternative to moussaka.

AUBERGINE AND TOMATO CHARLOTTE

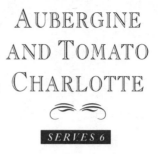

SERVES 6

INGREDIENTS

1 large aubergine, weighing about 450 g (1 lb)	8-10 tomatoes or 400 g (14 oz) can chopped tomatoes
salt and freshly ground black pepper	15 ml (1 tbs) chopped fresh basil or
60-120 ml (4-6 tbs) olive oil	2.5 ml (^{1}/2 tsp) dried basil
1 onion, chopped	250 ml (10 fl oz) natural yoghurt
1 garlic clove, crushed	150 g (5 oz) wheat-free breadcrumbs

1 Preheat the oven to 180°C/350°F/Gas 4.

2 Wash and slice the aubergines. Sprinkle with salt and leave to 'sweat' for 10 minutes. Rinse and drain well.

3 Meanwhile, heat 15 ml (1 tbs) oil in a pan, add the onion and garlic and cook for 5 minutes until the onion is lightly browned. Add the tomatoes and basil and season to taste with salt and pepper. Simmer for about 20 minutes until pulpy.

4 Heat about 30 ml (2 tbs) oil in a frying-pan and brown the aubergine slices on each side, brushing each slice with olive oil.

5 Use the aubergine slices to line the bottom and sides of a 1.5 L (2 pt) ovenproof dish. Add a layer of tomatoes, followed by a layer of yoghurt, then breadcrumbs. Repeat these layers again, then cover the top with a layer of aubergines. Cover with kitchen foil and bake for about 40 minutes.

6 Leave to stand in the dish or tin for a few minutes before turning out onto a warmed serving plate.

NUTRITIONAL INFORMATION (PER SERVING)
Energy 780 kJ/186 kcal ■ *Protein 4 g* ■ *Carbohydrate 19 g* ■ *Fat 11 g*

MUSHROOM AND SPINACH ROULADE

〜〜

SERVES 4

THIS IS A SPINACH omelette with a difference! For a quick cheesy filling, mix 60 ml (4 tbs) natural yoghurt with 175 g (6 oz) chive-flavoured cottage cheese and use as described below.

For a mouthwatering summer lunch, serve with a mixed tossed salad and a glass of white wine.

INGREDIENTS

450 g (1 lb) fresh spinach
4 eggs, separated
generous pinch of grated nutmeg

salt and freshly ground black pepper
30 ml (2 tbs) finely grated
Cheddar cheese

FILLING

30 ml (2 tbs) vegetable oil
1 onion, chopped
150 g (5 oz) button mushrooms, sliced

25 g (1 oz) cornflour
150 ml (5 fl oz) milk

1 Preheat the oven to 200°C/400°F/Gas 6. Line a 25 x 30 cm (10 x 12 in) Swiss roll tin with greaseproof paper and grease.

2 Remove the stalks from the spinach and wash well. Place in a saucepan with no extra water and cook over moderate heat for about 10 minutes. Drain and chop finely. Mix the egg yolks into the spinach with the nutmeg and salt and pepper to taste.

3 In a separate bowl, whisk the egg whites until stiff, then carefully fold into the spinach mixture. Pour immediately into the Swiss roll tin and bake in the oven for about 15 minutes until golden brown and puffed.

4 Meanwhile, make the filling. Heat the oil in a pan, add the onion and fry gently for 3 minutes until soft. Add the mushrooms and cook, stirring, for a further 2 minutes. Stir 30 ml (2 tbs) milk into the cornflour and add to the pan. Remove from the heat and gradually stir in the remaining milk, then return to the heat and cook, stirring continuously, until the filling thickens. Season with salt and pepper to taste.

5 Sprinkle the grated cheese onto a sheet of greaseproof paper and turn the spinach roulade onto it. Remove the greaseproof lining and spread the roulade with the mushroom filling. Carefully roll up from a short side and serve.

NUTRITIONAL INFORMATION (PER SERVING)
Energy 1100 kJ/263 kcal ■ Protein 14 g ■ Carbohydrate 12 g ■ Fat 18 g

LONG-GRAIN RICE is included in this vegetable soufflé to make a hearty all-in-one family supper. Rice flour is used to thicken the sauce, giving the soufflé a delicious flavour and texture.

No matter how inexperienced a cook you are this is one soufflé which is guaranteed not to sink on you!

SAVOURY VEGETABLE SOUFFLE

SERVES 4

INGREDIENTS

75 g (3 oz) long-grain rice
110 g (4 oz) broccoli,
broken into small florets

225 g (8 oz) can chopped tomatoes
50 g (2 oz) smoked ham

SAUCE

25 g (1 oz) margarine
60 ml (4 tbs) brown rice flour
300 ml (10 fl oz) milk
110 g (4 oz) Cheddar cheese, grated

15 g ($^1/_2$ oz) Parmesan cheese,
finely grated
3 eggs, separated
salt and freshly ground black pepper

1 Preheat the oven to 180°C/350°F/Gas 4; grease a 1.2 L (2 pt) soufflé dish. Rinse the rice under cold running water, then cook in boiling salted water for about 8-10 minutes until just tender and drain. Steam the broccoli until just tender.

2 To make the sauce, melt the margarine in a pan. Add the rice flour and cook for a few seconds, stirring. Remove from the heat and gradually stir in the milk. Return to the heat and cook, stirring continuously, until the sauce is thickened and smooth. Add the Cheddar and three-quarters of the Parmesan, and heat until melted. Season to taste with salt and pepper, then leave the sauce to cool for 5 minutes.

3 Meanwhile, drain the tomatoes and place in the bottom of the soufflé dish with the ham. Add the rice, then the broccoli.

4 Add the egg yolks to the cheese sauce and stir well. Whisk the egg whites until they form stiff peaks and fold into the sauce. Pour over the vegetables in the soufflé dish and mix slightly. Sprinkle the remaining Parmesan cheese over the top of the mixture and bake in the oven for 45 minutes until well risen and cooked through. Serve at once.

NUTRITIONAL INFORMATION (PER SERVING)
Energy 1805 kJ/432 kcal ■ Protein 22 g ■ Carbohydrate 34 g ■ Fat 24 g

SPOONBREAD WITH BOSTON BEANS

SERVES 4

A RECIPE WHICH hails from America's Deep South, spoonbread is a firm favourite all over the USA where it is served with a variety of interesting dishes. Made from cornmeal it is rather like a soufflé in texture, a perfect accompaniment to the tasty fibre-rich Boston beans.

INGREDIENTS

110 g (4 oz) cornmeal
450 ml (16 fl oz) milk
25 g (1 oz) margarine
or butter
15 ml (1 tbs) soft brown sugar

generous pinch of salt
1.5 ml ($^1/_4$ tsp) grated nutmeg
2.5 ml ($^1/_2$ tsp) gluten-free
baking powder
3 eggs, separated

BOSTON BEANS

15 ml (1 tbs) sunflower oil
1 onion, chopped
110 g (4 oz) ham, chopped
425 g (15 oz) can gluten-free
baked beans

5 ml (1 tsp) black treacle
2.5 ml ($^1/_2$ tsp) French mustard
2.5 ml ($^1/_2$ tsp) wine vinegar
5 ml (1 tsp) yeast extract

1 Preheat the oven to 200°C/400°F/Gas 6. Grease a 1.5 L (2 $^1/_2$ pt) soufflé dish.

2 Combine the cornmeal with the milk in a pan. Place over a moderate heat and bring to the boil, stirring continuously. Reduce the heat slightly and simmer for 3 minutes, until thick. Allow to cool for 5 minutes.

3 Add the margarine, sugar, salt, nutmeg and baking powder to the cornmeal mixture. Beat in the egg yolks, one at a time. Whisk the egg whites until stiff, then fold in. Pour into the prepared dish and bake in the oven for about 30 minutes until golden and risen.

4 Meanwhile, make the Boston beans. Heat the oil in a pan, add the onion and cook for 5 minutes until lightly golden. Add the ham and fry for 2 minutes, stirring. Stir in the baked beans, treacle, mustard, vinegar and yeast extract. Cook gently for 10 minutes, stirring frequently.

5 Serve the spoonbread as soon as it is cooked, accompanied by the Boston beans.

NUTRITIONAL INFORMATION (PER SERVING)
Energy 2190 kJ/524 kcal ■ Protein 27 g ■ Carbohydrate 58 g ■ Fat 22 g

THIS IS A GREAT all-in-one summery meal, perfect for salad lovers. A very flexible dish, the ingredients can be varied according to personal taste and availability. Diced avocado and roughly chopped nuts or crispy lean bacon make a good addition.

CHEF'S
SALAD

SERVES 2

INGREDIENTS

assorted lettuce leaves
2 hard-boiled eggs
6 cherry tomatoes
25 g (1 oz) Feta or Cheshire
cheese, cubed

8 black olives
6 radishes, cleaned
3 spring onions, chopped
sunflower seeds, to garnish

DRESSING

60 ml (4 tbs) olive oil
15 ml (1 tbs) white wine vinegar
1 garlic clove, crushed
7.5 ml (1/2 tbs) lemon juice
2.5 ml (1/2 tsp) French mustard
2.5 ml (1/2 tsp) sugar
15 ml (1 tbs) snipped chives
salt and freshly ground black pepper

CROUTONS

25 g (1 oz) margarine
2 slices wheat-free bread
generous pinch ground paprika

1 To make the croûtons, heat the margarine in a frying-pan, add the bread cubes and fry until evenly golden brown. Drain on absorbent kitchen paper and sprinkle with paprika and salt to taste. Allow to cool.

2 To make the dressing, whisk the olive oil with the vinegar, garlic, lemon juice, mustard, sugar and snipped chives. Season to taste with salt and pepper.

3 Place the lettuce leaves in a salad bowl with the hard-boiled eggs, tomatoes, cheese, black olives, radishes and spring onions. Toss well in the dressing and serve garnished with sunflower seeds and the croûtons.

NUTRITIONAL INFORMATION (PER SERVING)
Energy 2600 kJ/621 kcal ■ Protein 13 g ■ Carbohydrate 15 g ■ Fat 57 g

PICNICS & PACKED LUNCHES

CHICKEN DRUMSTICKS ARE always popular at picnics, not just because they are so tasty, but also because they are so easy to eat with the fingers.

Served with the crunchy sweetcorn salad, this is another recipe infused with the flavours of America's Deep South, just right for al fresco eating on a hot summer's day.

Pack the drumsticks into separate rigid containers to store and serve.

SOUTHERN - STYLE CHICKEN WITH SWEETCORN SALAD

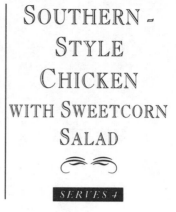

SERVES 4

INGREDIENTS

8 chicken drumsticks
2.5 ml (1/2 tsp) paprika
30 ml (2 tbs) vegetable oil
25 g (1 oz) cornflakes, crushed

110 g (4 oz) cornmeal or dried wheat-free breadcrumbs
salt and freshly ground black pepper

SWEETCORN SIDE SALAD

175 g (6 oz) long-grain rice
salt and freshly ground black pepper
45 ml (3 tbs) vegetable oil
15 ml (1 tbs) lemon juice
2.5 ml (1/2 tsp) ground ginger

200 g (7 oz) can sweetcorn and pimento, drained
2 celery sticks, sliced
200 g (7 oz) can pineapple chunks, drained
50 g (2 oz) unsalted peanuts

1 Preheat the oven to 200°C/400°F/Gas 6 and line a baking sheet with kitchen foil.

2 Wash the chicken drumsticks and pat dry with absorbent paper. Mix the paprika into the vegetable oil and brush onto the chicken. Mix the cornflakes into the cornmeal, season with salt and pepper and use to coat the drumsticks. Place on the prepared baking sheet and bake for about 25 minutes until golden. Leave to cool.

3 To make the salad, cook the rice in boiling water for about 12 minutes until tender. Drain and season with salt and pepper. Mix the vegetable oil with the lemon juice and ground ginger and stir into the rice while it is still warm. When the rice is cold, add the sweetcorn and pimento, celery, pineapple chunks and peanuts.

4 Pack the drumsticks and salad into separate rigid containers.

NUTRITIONAL INFORMATION (PER SERVING)
Energy 2735 kJ/654 kcal ■ Protein 19 g ■ Carbohydrate 87 g ■ Fat 28 g

SAVOURY BREAD PASTIES

MAKES 4

MADE WITH BREAD Mix rather than pastry these delicious pasties make a versatile meal or a hearty snack.

Not so delicate as their pastry counterparts, they travel well in a lunchbox without breaking up and can be made with a variety of meat or vegetable fillings.

INGREDIENTS

250 g (9 oz) Rite-Diet Brown
Bread Mix
5 g (1/2 sachet) dried yeast
125 ml (5 fl oz) tepid water

1 egg
15 ml (1 tbs) vegetable oil
1 egg, to glaze

FILLING

15 ml (1 tbs) vegetable oil
1 small onion, finely chopped
1/2 green pepper, de-seeded
and finely chopped
175 g (6 oz) minced turkey

15 ml (1 tbs) cornflour
200 g (7 oz) can chopped tomatoes
2.5 ml (1/2 tsp) dried mixed herbs
salt and freshly ground
black pepper

1 To make the filling, heat the oil in a saucepan, add the onion and pepper and cook for 3 minutes until the onion is softened. Add the turkey and continue to cook, stirring, until browned. Stir the cornflour into the tomatoes and add to the pan. Add the herbs and season to taste with salt and pepper. Simmer for about 15 minutes until a thick sauce is formed. Allow to cool.

2 In a bowl, blend the Bread Mix with the yeast. Add the water and egg and beat together to form a kneadable dough. Transfer the dough to a surface lightly floured with Bread Mix and knead until smooth. Roll out the dough and cut out 4 rounds, using a saucer as a guide.

3 Place some of the filling in the centre of each dough round. Brush the edges with egg glaze and fold in half. Seal the edges with a fork. Place on a greased baking tray and leave to prove in a warm place for 10 minutes. Preheat the oven to 200°C/400°F/ Gas 6.

4 Brush the pasties with egg glaze and bake in the oven for 10-15 minutes or until golden brown. Serve hot or cold.

NUTRITIONAL INFORMATION (PER SERVING)
Energy 1450 kJ/347 kcal ■ Protein 17 g ■ Carbohydrate 48 g ■ Fat 11 g

Tucked into pitta bread pockets (see recipe on page 132), these spicy meat-free falafel make easy-to-eat picnic fare. If you prefer to use dried chickpeas, you will need 110 g (4 oz) dried weight.

FALAFEL

MAKES 25

INGREDIENTS

*400 g (14 oz) can chickpeas, rinsed
and drained
50 g (2 oz) fresh wheat-free
breadcrumbs
1 egg, beaten
1 large onion, finely chopped
15 ml (1 tbs) finely chopped parsley*

*2 garlic cloves, crushed
50 g (2 oz) Glutafin Baking Mix
10 ml (2 tsp) cumin seeds, crushed
10 ml (2 tsp) coriander seeds,
crushed
5 ml (1 tsp) chilli powder
vegetable oil, for frying*

SALAD GARNISH

*2 tomatoes, sliced
1/2 onion, thinly sliced
1/4 crisp lettuce, shredded*

*1/4 cucumber, diced
10 black olives,
stoned (optional)*

1 Place the chickpeas in a food processor or blender and work until smooth. Add the breadcrumbs, egg, onion, parsley, garlic, Baking Mix and spices and stir well.

2 Lightly dust your hands with Baking Mix and shape the chickpea mixture into 25 walnut-sized balls.

3 Heat the vegetable oil in a deep-fat fryer, then fry the falafel in batches until golden brown. Drain on absorbent kitchen paper and allow to cool.

4 Pack the falafel and salad garnish into separate rigid containers.

NUTRITIONAL INFORMATION (PER SERVING)
Energy 150 kJ/36 kcal ▪ Protein 2 g ▪ Carbohydrate 5 g ▪ Fat 1 g

SAMOSAS

MAKES 20

AN INDIAN DELICACY now popular the world over, these crispy pastry triangles are equally tasty eaten hot or cold. They can be filled with succulent spicy vegetables as an alternative to meat.

INGREDIENTS

110 g (4 oz) Rite-Diet Flour Mix
pinch of salt
15 ml (1 tbs) vegetable oil

75 ml (3 fl oz) water
vegetable oil, for frying

FILLING

15 ml (1 tbs) vegetable oil
1 onion, chopped
225 g (8 oz) minced beef
2 garlic cloves, crushed
5 ml (1 tsp) ground cloves
10 ml (2 tsp) ground cumin

5-7.5 ml (1-1 1/2 tsp) chilli powder
10 ml (2 tsp) ground turmeric
15 ml (1 tbs) tomato purée
30 ml (2 tbs) lemon juice
25 g (1 oz) frozen peas
salt and freshly ground black pepper

1 Place the Flour Mix and salt in a bowl. Add the oil then stir in the water to make a soft dough. On a surface lightly floured with Flour Mix, knead the dough with the palm of your hand for 5-8 minutes until smooth. Set aside while you make the filling.

2 To make the filling, heat the oil in a pan, add the onion and cook for about 3 minutes until softened. Add the minced beef, garlic and spices and continue to cook, stirring, until the beef is browned. Drain off the fat. Add the tomato purée, lemon juice and peas and cook for a further 5 minutes. Remove from the heat and season with salt and pepper to taste.

3 Divide the dough into 10 equal-sized pieces and roll into balls. Flatten each ball and roll out thinly into 8 cm (5 in) circles on a lightly floured surface. Cut the circles in half, moisten the edges and fold into a cone shape. Spoon the filling into each cone until three-quarters full and dampen with water to seal well.

4 Heat the oil in a deep-fat fryer and fry the samosas for 3-4 minutes until golden brown. Drain on absorbent kitchen paper and serve hot or cold.

NUTRITIONAL INFORMATION (PER SERVING)
Energy 280 kJ/67 kcal ■ Protein 3 g ■ Carbohydrate 5 g ■ Fat 4 g

THESE DELICIOUS VEGETARIAN scotch eggs make an interesting addition to any lunch box. Packed with a crisp green salad and raw carrot sticks they provide a wholesome meal. To make breadcrumbs for the coating, dry off leftover bread in the oven, then work in a blender.

HERBY SCOTCH EGGS

MAKES 4

INGREDIENTS

4 eggs, hard-boiled
175 g (6 oz) fresh wheat-free breadcrumbs
50 g (2 oz) mixed nuts, finely chopped
2.5 ml (1/2 tsp) dried thyme
2.5 ml (1/2 tsp) dried parsley
75 g (3 oz) margarine
1 small onion, finely chopped

25 g (1 oz) mushrooms, finely chopped
1 egg, beaten
15 ml (1 tbs) tomato purée
10 ml (2 tsp) lemon juice
salt and freshly ground black pepper
cornflour, for rolling and dusting
vegetable oil, for deep frying

COATING

1 egg, beaten
45 ml (3 tbs) fine dry wheat-free breadcrumbs

1 Shell the hard-boiled eggs and roll in a little cornflour.

2 In a bowl, combine the fresh breadcrumbs with the chopped nuts and herbs. Melt the margarine and add to the bowl with the onion, mushrooms, beaten egg, tomato purée and lemon juice. Season with salt and pepper, then form into a firm ball. Divide the mixture into 4 and roll out to neat rounds on a board dusted with cornflour.

3 Wrap each egg in a round of mixture and seal well. Coat in beaten egg, then roll in breadcrumbs.

4 Heat the vegetable oil in a deep-fat fryer, add the coated eggs and fry for about 10 minutes until golden brown. Drain on absorbent kitchen paper and leave to cool.

NUTRITIONAL INFORMATION (PER SERVING)
Energy 2060kJ/492 kcal ■ Protein 16 g ■ Carbohydrate 23 g ■ Fat 38 g

STUFFED VINE LEAVES

MAKES 24

FOR A MEAT-FREE version of this Middle Eastern dish, increase the quantity of rice to 110 g (4 oz) and replace the meat with seedless raisins and pine nuts.

As well as being an excellent addition to a picnic hamper, stuffed vine leaves are also suitable for a pre-dinner snack or canapé.

INGREDIENTS

1 packet vine leaves
350 g (12 oz) minced lamb
1 onion, chopped
50 g (2 oz) long-grain rice
1 garlic clove, chopped
15 ml (1 tbs) tomato purée

juice of 1 lemon
10 ml (2 tsp) finely chopped mint
10 ml (2 tsp) finely chopped
parsley or dill
salt and freshly ground black pepper
10 ml (2 tsp) olive oil

1 Soak the vine leaves in a bowl of cold water to remove some of the salt. Drain, separate the leaves and leave to drain thoroughly on a wire rack. Bring a large saucepan of water to the boil, add the vine leaves and boil for 2 minutes. Drain and set aside.

2 To make the stuffing, combine the lamb, onion, uncooked rice, garlic, tomato purée, lemon juice, mint and parsley in a bowl. Season with salt and pepper and mix well.

3 Remove the hard stalk from the centre of each vine leaf, then place the leaves glossy side down. Place a scant tablespoon of the mixture at the stalk end of each leaf. Fold the side ends of the leaf over the stuffing and roll up into a small cigar-shaped roll.

4 Place the rolls in a large saucepan lined with spare vine leaves, closely packed together in rows. Add the olive oil and a little water. Weigh down the rolls with a plate. Cover with a lid and simmer for about 35 minutes. Leave to cool in the pan, then pack into a rigid container.

NUTRITIONAL INFORMATION (PER SERVING)
Energy 195 kJ/47 kcal ■ Protein 4 g ■ Carbohydrate 1 g ■ Fat 3 g

THESE CRISPY BACON rolls with their melt-in-the-mouth mushroom and hazelnut filling would be a welcome addition to any picnic.

Alternatively, make double or treble the quantity, pile onto a warmed serving plate and serve them hot as canapés at a drinks party.

HAZELNUT BACON ROLLS

≈ ≈

MAKES 12

INGREDIENTS

25 g (1 oz) margarine
1 large onion, chopped
110 g (4 oz) mushrooms, chopped
50 g (2 oz) fresh wheat-free breadcrumbs
25 g (1 oz) shelled hazelnuts, finely chopped

15 ml (1 tbs) finely chopped parsley
2.5 ml ($1/2$ tsp) dried thyme
2.5 ml ($1/2$ tsp) dried sage
salt and freshly ground black pepper
12 rashers streaky bacon, rinds removed
30 ml (2 tbs) vegetable oil

1 Preheat the oven to 190°C/375°F/Gas 5.

2 Melt the margarine in a large frying-pan, add the chopped onion and cook gently for about 5 minutes until softened. Add the mushrooms and cook for a further 2 minutes, then remove from the heat. Stir the breadcrumbs into the pan with the hazelnuts, parsley, thyme and sage. Season to taste with salt and pepper.

3 Stretch and flatten the bacon rashers on a board with the back of a knife. Place a portion of the nut and mushroom mixture on the end of one rasher and roll up firmly. Secure the roll with a wooden cocktail stick. Repeat with remaining bacon rashers.

4 Spread the bacon rolls out evenly on a baking tray, spoon over the oil and bake in the oven for 20-25 minutes.

5 Remove the cocktail sticks and leave to cool. Pack in a rigid container.

NUTRITIONAL INFORMATION (PER SERVING)
Energy 716 kJ/171 kcal ▪ *Protein 5 g* ▪ *Carbohydrate 4 g* ▪ *Fat 15 g*

TANGY FISH SALAD

SERVES 4

SMOKED FISH IS combined with cooked pasta and a fruity salad to make a nutritious summery meal, ideal for outdoor eating. For a quick version, try using tuna or some other variety of tinned fish instead of the smoked cod.

INGREDIENTS

450 g (1 lb) smoked cod fillets
110 g (4 oz) wheat-free
macaroni
150 ml (5 fl oz) water
1/2 green pepper, de-seeded
and chopped
2 celery sticks, chopped
1 red apple, diced

25 g (1 oz) walnuts or mixed
nuts, chopped
150 ml (5 fl oz) natural yoghurt
15 ml (1 tbs) mayonnaise
juice and finely grated rind
of 1/2 lemon
salt and freshly ground black pepper
lettuce leaves

fresh parsley sprigs and
tomato wedges, to garnish

1 Place the cod in a pan and cover with the water. Bring to simmering point, cover and poach gently until cooked.

2 Cook the pasta in boiling salted water for about 10 minutes until *al dente*, then drain, rinse and drain again.

3 In a bowl, combine the green pepper with the celery, red apple, chopped nuts, yoghurt, mayonnaise and lemon juice and rind. Stir in the fish and pasta, then season to taste with salt and pepper.

4 Arrange the salad on a bed of lettuce and pack in a rigid container. Garnish with parsley and tomato wedges.

NUTRITIONAL INFORMATION (PER SERVING)
Energy 1345 kJ/321 kcal ■ Protein 25 g ■ Carbohydrate 30 g ■ Fat 12 g

TOMATO SHELLS MAKE handy containers for salad mixtures. In this fresh-tasting recipe, prawns and avocado are hidden beneath a cheesy layer to make a colourful and tasty addition to any picnic.

Make sure that you select tomatoes that are large and firm enough to hold their filling well.

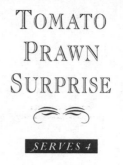

TOMATO PRAWN SURPRISE

SERVES 4

INGREDIENTS

4 large tomatoes
1 large avocado
110 g (4 oz) peeled cooked prawns
175 g (6 oz) cottage cheese

15 ml (1 tbs) snipped chives
a few drops of Tabasco sauce
paprika, to garnish

DRESSING

45 ml (3 tbs) olive oil
15 ml (1 tbs) lemon juice
5 ml (1 tsp) wheat-free French mustard

15 ml(1 tbs) finely chopped coriander
pinch of sugar
salt and freshly ground black pepper

1 Slice off the tops of the tomatoes, then scoop out the flesh and seeds and discard.

2 To make the dressing, blend the olive oil with the lemon juice, mustard, coriander, sugar and salt and pepper.

3 Peel, stone and cube the avocado and place in a bowl with the prawns. Pour over the dressing and mix gently. Three-quarters fill the tomato shells with the prawn mixture.

4 Mix the snipped chives into the cottage cheese and flavour with Tabasco sauce. Spoon into the tomato shells to cover the prawn mixture. Garnish with a sprinkling of paprika and pack in a rigid container.

NUTRITIONAL INFORMATION (PER SERVING)
Energy 1221 kJ/292 kcal ▪ Protein 14 g ▪ Carbohydrate 3 g ▪ Fat 25 g

MIDDLE EASTERN BUCKWHEAT SALAD

SERVES 4-6

A WHEAT-FREE version of the classic Middle Eastern dish Tabbouleh, this unusual salad combines roasted buckwheat with crunchy raw vegetables and a generous quantity of herbs. Tossed in a piquant garlic-flavoured dressing, it is excellent served with flans and cold meats.

One of the main ingredients of the dressing is tahini, a delicious paste made from ground sesame seeds.

INGREDIENTS

175 g (6 oz) roasted whole buckwheat
2 tomatoes, diced
2 celery sticks, chopped
3 spring onions, chopped
1 red pepper, de-seeded and diced
45 ml (3 tbs) finely chopped coriander
or parsley
15 ml (1 tbs) chopped mint

DRESSING

30 ml (2 tbs) olive oil
30 ml (2 tbs) lemon juice
1 garlic clove, crushed
15 ml (1 tbs) tahini
salt and freshly ground black pepper
15 ml (1 tbs) black olives,
fresh coriander sprigs and
lemon wedges, to garnish

1 To make the dressing, beat together the oil, lemon juice, tahini and garlic, then season generously with salt and pepper.

2 Bring a pan of salted water to the boil, add the buckwheat and boil for 5-6 minutes. Drain and rinse under cold running water. Drain well.

3 Place the buckwheat in a bowl, add the dressing and toss well. Stir in the tomatoes, celery, spring onion, red pepper and herbs. Mix thoroughly.

4 Pack in a rigid container and garnish with black olives, lemon wedges and a sprig of coriander.

NUTRITIONAL INFORMATION (PER SERVING)
Energy 800 kJ/191 kcal ■ Protein 3 g ■ Carbohydrate 31 g ■ Fat 7 g

THIS COLOURFUL, CRISP salad will' add texture and interest to any picnic spread and is similar to the German favourite, coleslaw.

For an interesting variation in flavour as well as texture, replace the grapes with a handful of unsalted cashews or peanuts and raisins.

CRUNCHY CABBAGE SALAD

≈ ≈

SERVES 4

INGREDIENTS

110 g (4 oz) white cabbage, shredded
110 g (4 oz) red cabbage, shredded
110 g (4 oz) grapes, de-seeded
2 celery sticks, sliced

1 carrot, grated
15 g (1/2 oz) sunflower seeds
salt and freshly ground black pepper

DRESSING

30 ml (2 tbs) apple juice
15 ml (1 tbs) sunflower oil
15 ml (1 tbs) lemon juice

2.5 ml (1/2 tsp) wheat-free
wholegrain mustard

1 To make the dressing, blend the apple juice with the oil, lemon juice and mustard. Season to taste with salt and pepper.

2 Place the cabbage in a bowl. Halve the grapes and add to the bowl with the celery, carrot, sunflower seeds and salt and pepper to taste.

3 Pour the dressing over the salad and toss to coat well. Pack into a rigid container.

NUTRITIONAL INFORMATION (PER SERVING)
Energy 318 kJ/92 kcal ■ Protein 2 g ■ Carbohydrate 8 g ■ Fat 6 g

CHEESE BITES

MAKES 25

HEALTHY AND VERY tasty, these savoury biscuits are ideal for packed lunches. For added fibre, use soya or rice bran or sugarbeet fibre. To make crispy canapés to hand round at a drinks party, use a variety of fancy pastry cutters.

INGREDIENTS

75 g (3 oz) Cheddar cheese, grated
30 ml (2 tbs) finely grated Parmesan cheese
75 g (3 oz) margarine

110 g (4 oz) Glutafin Baking Mix
25 g (1 oz) wheat-free fibre or bran
1 egg, beaten
15 g (1/2 oz) sesame seeds

1 Preheat the oven to 190°C/375°F/Gas 5.

2 In a large bowl, beat together the cheese and margarine. Work in the Baking Mix and fibre to make a kneadable dough. Roll out the dough on a surface lightly floured with Baking Mix and cut into rounds using a 4 cm (1 1/2 in) pastry cutter.

3 Transfer the rounds to a greased baking sheet. Brush with beaten egg and sprinkle with sesame seeds. Bake in the oven for 10-15 minutes or until golden brown.

4 Cool the biscuits and store in an airtight container.

NUTRITIONAL INFORMATION (PER SERVING)
Energy 285 kJ/68 kcal ■ Protein 2 g ■ Carbohydrate 4 g ■ Fat 5 g

THICKENED WITH A variety of root vegetables, this warming soup is just the job for a sporting event on a chilly day. If wished, garnish with crumbled, crisply-fried bacon for added texture. Try using parsnip instead of celeriac when you want to ring the changes, and serve at the table from a huge tureen for a hearty lunch.

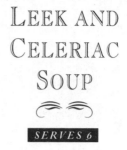

LEEK AND CELERIAC SOUP

SERVES 6

INGREDIENTS

15 ml (1 tbs) vegetable oil
2 leeks, sliced
1 celeriac, weighing about 450 g (1 lb), chopped
225 g (8 oz) carrots, sliced
1 potato, diced

900 ml (1 ¹/2 pt) vegetable or chicken stock
2.5 ml (¹/2 tsp) grated nutmeg
salt and freshly ground black pepper
150 ml (5 fl oz) milk

1 Heat the oil in a large pan, add the leeks and cook for 5 minutes until just softened. Add the celeriac, carrots and potato and cook for a further 5 minutes, stirring occasionally.

2 Add the stock, nutmeg and salt and pepper to taste. Bring to the boil, then reduce the heat, cover and simmer for about 30 minutes. Allow to cool slightly, then purée in a food processor or blender until smooth.

3 Return the purée to the pan, add the milk and heat through. Adjust the seasoning and pour into a suitable flask.

NUTRITIONAL INFORMATION (PER SERVING)
Energy 345 kJ/82 kcal ▪ *Protein 3 g* ▪ *Carbohydrate 9 g* ▪ *Fat 4 g*

DESSERTS

CREPES SUZETTE IS a French dish that has become almost synonymous with sophisticated dining in recent years.

These lighter-than-air crêpes are flamed with liqueur for a spectacular finish to a memorable meal.

CREPES
SUZETTE

SERVES 6

INGREDIENTS

110 g (4 oz) Glutafin Baking Mix
2 eggs, beaten

110 g (4 fl oz) milk
vegetable oil, for frying

SAUCE

50 g (2 oz) butter
50 g (2 oz) caster sugar

150 ml (5 fl oz) orange juice
45 ml (3 tbs) orange liqueur

1 Place the Baking Mix in a mixing bowl. Make a well in the centre and add the eggs and 30 ml (2 tbs) milk. Beat with a wooden spoon to form a smooth batter, then gradually work in the remaining milk.

2 Heat a little oil in a small non-stick pan. Remove from the heat and pour off any excess oil. Pour in about 30 ml (2 tbs) batter, tilting the pan to spread the batter evenly over the pan base. Cook over a moderate heat until the top is beginning to look dry and the underside is golden. Loosen the edge with a palette knife, then flip over and cook the other side for 20-30 seconds until golden. Slide onto a sheet of greaseproof paper. Make 10-12 more crêpes, interleaving them with greaseproof paper.

3 Melt the butter in a large flameproof dish, then stir in the sugar and the orange juice. Add the crêpes to the dish, coating them well in the sauce and folding into quarters. Add the liqueur. Heat gently and light with a taper to serve flamed.

NUTRITIONAL INFORMATION (PER SERVING)
Energy 1015 kJ/243 kcal ▪ *Protein 4 g* ▪ *Carbohydrate 27 g* ▪ *Fat 14 g*

FRENCH FRUIT FLAN

SERVES 6

A FRUIT-TOPPED flan makes a glamorous dessert and you can vary the fruit according to seasonal availability. This recipe works equally well with peaches and raspberries.

Gluten-free pastry lacks the 'stretchiness' of ordinary dough, but it will not shrink.

INGREDIENTS

300 ml (10 fl oz) milk
30 ml (2 tbs) custard powder
15 ml (1 tbs) sugar
45-60 ml (3-4 tbs) fromage frais
10 ml (2 tsp) sherry

225 g (8 oz) strawberries
2 kiwi fruit, sliced
2 nectarines, sliced or halved
60 ml (4 tbs) redcurrant jelly
5 ml (1 tsp) liqueur

PASTRY

175 g (6 oz) Glutafin Baking Mix
75 g (3 oz) margarine
25 g (1 oz) caster sugar

15-30 ml (1-2 tbs) water
drop of vanilla essence

1 Preheat the oven to 190°C/375°F/Gas 5.

2 To make the pastry, put the Baking Mix and margarine in a mixing bowl and lightly rub together with your fingertips until the mixture resembles fine breadcrumbs. Stir in the sugar, then add the water and vanilla essence and cut in with a knife. Bring together by hand to form a soft dough, then knead gently on a surface lightly floured with Baking Mix and roll out between two sheets of greaseproof paper (this will make it easier to handle).

3 Transfer the pastry using the paper to a 20 cm (8 in) flan ring and gently press into place. Trim with a knife, then cover the base with greaseproof paper and a handful of dried beans. Bake for about 10 minutes until golden brown. Remove paper and beans and bake for a further 5 minutes. Leave to cool.

4 In a pan, bring the milk to simmering point. Combine a little of the hot milk with the custard powder and sugar to make a paste, then return to the pan of milk. Cook, stirring, until thick and leave to cool. Once cold, mix in the fromage frais and sherry. Pour into the cold flan case.

5 Slice the strawberries. Peel and slice the kiwi fruit and nectarines. Arrange the fruit on top of the custard. Melt the redcurrant jelly with the liqueur in a small pan and heat gently, stirring, until smooth. Brush over the fruit and allow to set before serving.

NUTRITIONAL INFORMATION (PER SERVING)
Energy 1140 kJ/272 kcal ▪ *Protein 4 g* ▪ *Carbohydrate 37 g* ▪ *Fat 13 g*

STRAWBERRY SHORTBREAD GALETTE

SERVES 8

A DELICIOUS DESSERT for a special occasion, strawberries on a bed of crème patissière with a crunchy shortbread base is hard to beat.

For everyday eating leave off the creamy topping and make plain or chocolate-dipped shortbread fans or fingers for a most acceptable teatime treat.

INGREDIENTS

250 g (9 oz) Glutafin Baking Mix
110 g (4 oz) icing sugar
110 g (4 oz) ground rice
150 g (5 oz) butter

5 ml (1 tsp) finely grated lemon rind
caster sugar, for sprinkling
1 punnet of fresh strawberries, sliced

CREME PATISSIERE

1 egg and 2 egg yolks
50 g (2 oz) cornflour
50 g (2 oz) sugar

2-3 drops vanilla essence
300 ml (10 fl oz) milk
125 ml (4 1/2 fl oz) whipping cream

1 Preheat the oven to 170°C/325°F/Gas 3. Line two 20 cm (8 in) shallow cake tins with greaseproof paper.

2 Combine the Baking Mix, icing sugar and ground rice in a mixing bowl. Rub in the butter with your fingertips until the mixture resembles breadcrumbs. Add the lemon rind and work the mixture into a dough that leaves the bowl clean. Divide in half.

3 Roll out the pieces of dough into two 20 cm (8 in) rounds and press into the lined cake tins. Mark one round into 12 wedges. Prick with a fork and bake the two rounds for about 40 minutes until light golden.

4 Cut the marked shortbread into wedges while still warm, then sprinkle with caster sugar and leave to cool on a wire rack. Remove the other round from the cake tin and leave to cool.

5 To make crème patissière, whisk together the egg, egg yolks, cornflour, sugar and vanilla essence in a bowl. Heat the milk to simmering point, then add 30 ml (2 tbs) of hot milk to the egg mixture. Pour the egg mixture into the pan of milk and cook over a low heat, stirring continuously, until thick. Leave to cool. When cold, fold in the whipped cream.

6 To assemble, spread crème patissière over the shortbread circle and cover with strawberry slices. Angle the shortbread wedges around the cake, placing extra strawberries between each wedge. Chill until required.

NUTRITIONAL INFORMATION (PER SERVING)
Energy 2100 kJ/502 kcal ■ *Protein 6 g* ■ *Carbohydrate 65 g* ■ *Fat 26 g*

PROFITEROLES WITH CHOCOLATE SAUCE

⌒⌒

MAKES 12

LIGHT AS AIR profiteroles filled with whipped cream and covered with dark chocolate sauce are many people's idea of heaven. The gluten-free version is every bit as good as the the original, and quite as sinful!

The cream-filled profiteroles can be open-frozen on a tray. Keep in a bag or container until needed, defrost and enjoy with chocolate sauce.

INGREDIENTS

50 g (2 oz) margarine
125 ml (4 1/2 fl oz) water
65 g (2 1/2 oz) Rite-Diet Flour Mix

2 eggs
150 ml (5 fl oz) whipped cream,
for filling

CHOCOLATE SAUCE

75 g (3 oz) plain chocolate
25 g (1 oz) sugar
25 g (1 oz) Rite-Diet Flour Mix
or cornflour

300 ml (10 fl oz) milk
15 g (1/2 oz) margarine

1 Preheat the oven to 220°C/425°F/Gas 7. Grease a baking sheet. Place the margarine and water in a pan and bring to the boil. Remove from the heat. Add all the Flour Mix at once and beat well until the mixture forms a smooth ball, leaving sides of the pan clean. Allow to cool slightly, then beat in the egg a little at a time, until smooth and glossy.

2 Place teaspoons of the mixture on the prepared baking sheet and bake in the oven for about 25 minutes until well risen and golden - do not open the oven door for at least 20 minutes. Make a slit in the side of each profiterole and leave to cool on a wire rack.

3 To make the sauce, place the chocolate in a bowl over a pan of hot water. Combine the sugar and Flour Mix with 45 ml (3 tbs) milk. Place the rest of the milk in pan, bring to the boil and stir into the sugar mixture. Mix in the margarine. Return the sauce to the pan and simmer, stirring continuously, until thickened. Stir in the melted chocolate.

4 Fill the profiteroles with whipped cream, pile onto individual plates and pour over the chocolate sauce. Serve at once.

NUTRITIONAL INFORMATION (PER SERVING)
Energy 760 kJ/182 kcal ■ Protein 3 g ■ Carbohydrate 14 g ■ Fat 13 g

IF GROUND HAZELNUTS are not available, buy whole nuts and grind them finely in an electric grinder. If you prefer to skin the nuts before grinding, roast them in a medium oven for 15 minutes until browned, then place in a soft tea-towel and rub off the skins.

PEACH NUT MERINGUE

SERVES 6

INGREDIENTS

200 ml (7 fl oz) Greek yoghurt
400 g (14 oz) can peach
slices, drained

15 ml (1 tbs) Kirsch (optional)
25 g (1 oz) whole hazelnuts,
to decorate

HAZELNUT MERINGUE

4 egg whites
225 g (8 oz) caster sugar
50 g (2 oz) ground hazelnuts

1 Heat the oven to 150°C/300°F/Gas 2. Grease and line with greaseproof paper two 23 cm (9 in) sandwich cake tins or mark two 23 cm (9 in) circles on lined baking trays.

2 To make the meringue, place the egg whites in a large bowl and whisk until stiff. Gradually whisk in the sugar, a little at a time, whisking well after each addition. Fold in the ground hazelnuts with a metal spoon, then divide the meringue between the prepared tins, smoothing the surface, or spoon onto the circles marked on baking trays. Bake in the oven for about 25 minutes until set and lightly browned. Leave to cool, then carefully turn out onto a wire rack and peel off the lining paper.

3 Reserve 4-5 peach slices for decoration, then purée the rest in a food processor or blender. Stir the purée and Kirsch, if using, into half the yoghurt, then spread over one meringue layer. Top with the second meringue layer.

4 Spread the remaining yoghurt over the meringue, then decorate the edge with the slivers of the reserved peach slices and whole hazelnuts. Refrigerate for up to 2 hours until ready to serve.

NUTRITIONAL INFORMATION (PER SERVING)
Energy 1384 kJ/331 kcal ■ *Protein 6 g* ■ *Carbohydrate 57 g* ■ *Fat 10 g*

RASPBERRY CHARLOTTE

SERVES 8

THIS DESSERT CAN also be made with canned raspberries. When using canned raspberries, replace half the milk with the canned syrup.

For a special treat, why not try substituting fresh strawberries or blackberries when in season.

INGREDIENTS

450 g (1 lb) raspberries
15-30 ml (1-2 tbs) icing sugar, sifted
15 ml (1 tbs) powdered gelatine
60 ml (4 tbs) water

2 eggs, separated
175 g (6 oz) sugar
450 ml (17 fl oz) milk
300 ml (10 fl oz) double cream

SPONGE FINGERS

2 eggs
2-3 drops vanilla essence
50 g (2 oz) caster sugar

65 g (2 1/2 oz) Rite-Diet Flour Mix
caster sugar, for sprinkling

1 Preheat the oven to 220°C/425°F/Gas 7. Grease 2 baking sheets.

2 To make the sponge fingers, whisk the eggs, vanilla essence and sugar together in a bowl placed over a pan of simmering water until the mixture is really thick and creamy and leaves a heavy trail when the whisk is lifted. Remove from the heat and gently fold in the Flour Mix. Place the mixture in a piping bag fitted with a 1 cm (1/2 in) plain nozzle and pipe into 10 cm (4 in) long fingers, spacing them well apart on the prepared baking sheets. Bake for 4 minutes until an even pale brown. Transfer to a wire rack, sprinkle with caster sugar and leave to cool.

3 Press the raspberries through a nylon sieve with a wooden spoon, or purée in a food processor or blender, then sieve. Sweeten to taste with icing sugar. Soak the gelatine in the water.

4 Arrange the sponge fingers upright around an 18 cm (7 in) charlotte mould or soufflé dish.

5 Whisk the egg yolks and sugar together until creamy. Heat the milk in a pan until nearly boiling, then whisk into the egg mixture with the vanilla essence. Return to the pan and cook gently, stirring, until thickened. Dissolve the soaked gelatine over hot water until transparent, then add to the custard in a thin stream, stirring well. Leave to cool, stirring occasionally.

6 Stir the puréed raspberries into the cooled custard. Whip the cream until thick, then fold in. Whisk the egg whites until stiff, then fold into the raspberry mixture. Chill for about 1 hour until almost set.

7 Spoon the raspberry mixture into the prepared mould and chill until completely set. Trim the sponge fingers level with the filling.

8 To serve, dip the mould in boiling water for a few seconds, then turn the charlotte out onto a plate. Decorate with fresh raspberries, if wished.

NUTRITIONAL INFORMATION (PER SERVING)
Energy 985 kJ/235 kcal ▪ *Protein 8 g* ▪ *Carbohydrate 47 g* ▪ *Fat 3 g*

CHOCOLATE CHESTNUT ROULADE

SERVES 6

THIS TEMPTING DESSERT would be ideal for serving at Christmas as an alternative to the traditional Yule Log, although the delicious flavours of chocolate and chestnut go well together at any time of year.

As it is filled with fromage frais rather than cream, it is not really as naughty as it looks!

INGREDIENTS

6 eggs, separated
150 g (5 oz) caster sugar
50 g (2 oz) gluten-free cocoa powder
5 ml (1 tsp) instant coffee powder

1-2 drops vanilla essence
icing sugar, for dusting
marrons glacé, to decorate
(optional)

CHESTNUT FILLING

110 g (4 oz) can chestnut purée
150 g (5 oz) fromage frais

50 g (2 oz) caster sugar
15 ml (1 tbs) brandy

1 Preheat the oven to 180°C/350°F/Gas 4. Grease a 25 x 30 cm (10 x 12 in) Swiss roll tin and line with greaseproof paper.

2 In a bowl, whisk the egg yolks until they start to thicken. Add the sugar and whisk until slightly thicker, then stir in the cocoa powder, coffee powder and vanilla essence. In a separate bowl whisk the egg whites to form soft peaks and carefully fold into the chocolate mixture. Pour into the prepared tin and bake in the oven for about 15-20 minutes until risen and springy to the touch.

3 Meanwhile, make the filling. Beat the chestnut purée to soften slightly, then mix in the fromage frais. Mix in the sugar and the brandy.

4 Allow the cooked cake to cool in the tin, then turn out onto greaseproof paper that has been dusted with icing sugar. Peel off the lining paper, spread the chestnut filling over the cake and roll up. Sift more icing sugar along the length of the roll and decorate with marrons glacé, if wished.

NUTRITIONAL INFORMATION (PER SERVING)
Energy 1310 kJ/313 kcal ■ Protein 11 g ■ Carbohydrate 44 g ■ Fat 11 g

IF WISHED, REMOVE the pith from the orange once the rind has been used for grating and cut the flesh into slices or segments for decorating the finished dish. For a sophisticated touch, add some orange-flavoured liqueur once the rice is cooked.

ORANGE RICE CONDE

SERVES 8

INGREDIENTS

600 ml (1 pt) milk
finely grated rind of 1 orange
110 g (4 oz) pudding rice

35 g (1 1/2 oz) powdered gelatine
30 ml (2 tbs) water
150 ml (5 fl oz) whipping cream

1 Place the milk in a pan with the orange rind and bring to the boil. Add the rice and bring back to the boil, stirring continuously. Lower the heat slightly and simmer for 45 minutes or until the rice is tender. Soak the gelatine in the water, then dissolve over a bowl of hot water. Add to the rice in a thin stream, stirring. Leave to cool.

2 When the rice is nearly cold, whip the cream until stiff then fold into the rice mixture. Pour into a round mould and leave for at least 2 hours to set.

3 To unmould the rice condé, place the mould in a bowl of hot water for a few seconds to loosen the edges and turn out onto a flat plate.

NUTRITIONAL INFORMATION (PER SERVING)
Energy 965 kJ/231 kcal ▪ Protein 4 g ▪ Carbohydrate 31 g ▪ Fat 11 g

TIRAMISU

SERVES 8

USING WHEAT-FREE sponge fingers, this divine Italian creation is now back on the menu for anyone suffering from gluten intolerance. It has the advantage that it can be made hours in advance of a special meal.

INGREDIENTS

30 ml (2 tbs) soft brown muscavado sugar
3 eggs
2 x 250 g (9 oz) mascarpone or low-fat soft cheese

50 g (2 oz) grated chocolate
150 ml (5 fl oz) strong black coffee, cooled
45 ml (3 tbs) Marsala or Tia Maria (optional)

SPONGE FINGERS

2 eggs
2-3 drops vanilla essence

50 g (2 oz) caster sugar
65 g (2 1/2 oz) Rite-Diet Flour Mix

1 Preheat the oven to 220°C/425°F/Gas 7. Grease two baking sheets. To make the sponge fingers, whisk the eggs, vanilla essence and sugar together in a bowl placed over a pan of simmering water until the mixture is really thick and creamy and leaves a heavy trail when the whisk is lifted. Remove from the heat and gently fold in the Flour Mix.

2 Place the mixture in a piping bag fitted with a 1 cm (1/2 in) plain nozzle and pipe into 8 cm (3 in) long fingers, spacing them well apart on the prepared baking sheets - there should be 14 fingers in all. Bake for 6 minutes until an even pale brown. Transfer to a wire rack and leave to cool.

3 To make the Tiramisu, place the sugar, eggs and cheese in a mixing bowl. Reserve 15 ml (1 tbs) grated chocolate and add the rest to the bowl. Beat well.

4 Mix the coffee with the Marsala, if using. Dip the sponge fingers into the coffee mixture and lay half of them in a suitable dish. Cover with half the cream, followed by the remaining sponge fingers and ending with a layer of cream.

5 Sprinkle with the remaining chocolate and chill for a few hours before serving.

NUTRITIONAL INFORMATION (PER SERVING)
Energy 1765 kJ/422 kcal ■ Protein 7 g ■ Carbohydrate 21 g ■ Fat 35 g

AN ATTRACTIVE VARIATION on Summer Pudding, these individual puddings are baked in ramekin dishes and filled with a refreshing mixture of apple purée and dried apricots.

Serve piping hot with custard made from skimmed milk or Greek yoghurt, fromage frais, single cream or smetana.

APRICOT AND APPLE PUDDINGS

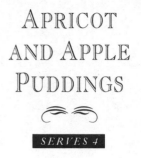

SERVES 4

INGREDIENTS

450 g (1 lb) cooking apples
30 ml (2 tbs) water
50 g (2 oz) demerara sugar
50 g (2 oz) no-need-to-soak dried apricots, chopped

finely grated rind and juice of
1/2 lemon
10 thin slices wheat-free bread
110 g (4 oz) margarine, melted
45 ml (3 tbs) single cream or smetana, to serve

1 Preheat the oven to 190°C/375°F/Gas 5.

2 Peel, core and chop the apples, then place in a pan with the water and sugar. Cook over gentle heat, stirring occasionally, until the apples are soft. Drain off surplus liquid and mash to a purée, then transfer to a bowl. Stir in the apricots and lemon rind and juice.

3 Remove the crusts from the bread. Cut out 4 circles of bread to use for lining the bases of 4 ramekin dishes. Cut out 4 more circles to use as lids and cut the remaining bread into strips to line the sides. Dip the bread bases and strips into the melted margarine and use to line 4 ramekin dishes. Spoon the fruit mixture into each ramekin and spread evenly. Dip the bread lids into the melted margarine and press on top of the filling.

4 Bake in the oven for 25 minutes or until the bread is crispy and golden brown. Turn out onto individual plates and spoon the cream over each pudding to serve.

NUTRITIONAL INFORMATION (PER SERVING)
Energy 1860 kJ/444 kcal ▪ *Protein 4 g* ▪ *Carbohydrate 54 g* ▪ *Fat 25 g*

Fruit and Spice Bread Pudding

SERVES 6

AN IDEAL WAY of using up left-over bread, this scrumptious pudding is delicious served hot with thin custard or fromage frais. When cooled and cut into wedges, it also makes an excellent addition to a packed lunch. For convenience, the wedges can be frozen individually and used as required.

INGREDIENTS

225 g (8 oz) wheat-free bread
150 ml (5 fl oz) milk
175 g (6 oz) mixed dried fruit
50 g (2 oz) margarine, melted
75 g (3 oz) fromage frais
50 g (2 oz) demerara sugar

10 ml (2 tsp) gluten-free mixed spice
finely grated rind of 1 lemon
1 egg, beaten
demerara sugar, for sprinkling
pinch of grated nutmeg

1 Preheat the oven to 180°C/350°F/Gas 4. Grease a 1.2 L (2 pt) pie dish or two 18 cm (7 in) square tins.

2 Place the bread in a mixing bowl and break up into small pieces. Add the milk and leave to soak for about 20 minutes. Beat out any lumps with a fork, then stir in the mixed fruit, melted margarine, fromage frais, sugar, spice and lemon rind. Mix well. Stir in the egg and, if necessary, add a little water to make a pouring consistency.

3 Pour the mixture into the pie dish or square tins. Sprinkle the sugar and nutmeg over the surface and bake in the oven for about 1 hour until firm and brown. Cut and serve, or leave to cool.

NUTRITIONAL INFORMATION (PER SERVING)
Energy 1100 kJ/263 kcal ■ Protein 5 g ■ Carbohydrate 43 g ■ Fat 9 g

APPLE AND BLACKBERRY MUESLI CRUMBLE

⌒⌒

SERVES 4

THE CRUNCHY TOPPING to this dish is both a healthy and tasty alternative to a traditional crumble.

The apple and blackberry filling may be gently stewed before adding the topping, so that the fully assembled crumble will only need to be baked for about 20 minutes in the oven. A generous dollop of creamy fromage frais or Greek yoghurt completes a real treat.

INGREDIENTS

450 g (1 lb) apples
110 g (4 oz) blackberries
15 ml (1 tbs) water

15 ml (1 tbs) sugar
fromage frais, to serve

TOPPING

50 g (2 oz) cornmeal
25 g (1 oz) rice flour
40 g (1 1/2 oz) margarine
15 g (1/2 oz) cornflakes,
  lightly crushed

15 g (1/2 oz) sultanas
15 g (1/2 oz) mixed nuts,
  roughly chopped
25 g (1 oz) demerara sugar

1 Preheat the oven to 190°C/375°F/Gas 5.

2 Peel, core and slice the apples, then place in an ovenproof dish. Gently stir in the blackberries, water and sugar.

3 To make the topping, place the cornmeal and rice flour in a mixing bowl. Add the margarine and rub together until the mixture resembles breadcrumbs. Stir in the cornflakes, sultanas, mixed nuts and demerara sugar, then spoon over the apples and blackberries.

4 Cook in the oven for 30 minutes until the topping is golden. Serve hot or cold with fromage frais.

NUTRITIONAL INFORMATION (PER SERVING)
Energy 1140 kJ/273 kcal ■ *Protein 4 g* ■ *Carbohydrate 42 g* ■ *Fat 11 g*

QUEEN OF PUDDINGS

SERVES 4

TOPPED WITH A crispy melt-in-the-mouth meringue layer, Queen of Puddings lives up to the grandeur of its name. When you serve up the wheat-free version of this classic pudding, both adults and children will be clamouring for more!

INGREDIENTS

75 g (3 oz) fresh wheat-free
breadcrumbs
300 ml (10 fl oz) milk
15 g (1/2 oz) margarine
15 g (1/2 oz) sugar

grated rind of 1/2 lemon or 2-3 drops
vanilla essence
2 egg yolks
30-45 ml (2-3 tbs) red jam

MERINGUE TOPPING

2 egg whites
75 g (3 oz) caster sugar

1 Preheat the oven to 180°C/350°F/Gas 4. Grease a 600 ml (1 pt) pie dish.

2 Crumble the bread by hand or in a blender. Place the milk and margarine in a pan and bring to the boil. Add the breadcrumbs, sugar and lemon rind, then cover the pan and leave to soak for 20 minutes. Beat in the egg yolks and turn the mixture into the prepared pie dish.

3 Bake for 20 minutes until just set and remove from the oven. Spread the jam over the breadcrumb mixture.

4 To make the meringue topping, whisk the egg whites until stiff, then whisk in 10 ml (2 tsp) sugar. Fold in the rest of the sugar with a metal spoon. Pile the meringue on top of the layer of jam and return to the oven for about 10 minutes until the meringue is crisp.

NUTRITIONAL INFORMATION (PER SERVING)
Energy 1155 kJ/276 kcal ▪ Protein 7 g ▪ Carbohydrate 42 g ▪ Fat 10 g

THIS IS A GREAT standby dessert and is delicious served with poached or canned fruit. If you are watching your fat intake, replace half the cream with yoghurt, and to cut down sugar, make sure any canned fruit you may be using is in natural juice rather than heavy syrup. The ice cream can be made in large quantities.

CRUNCHY BROWN BREAD ICE - CREAM

SERVES 10

INGREDIENTS

75 g (3 oz) fresh wheat-free
brown breadcrumbs
75 g (3 oz) demerara sugar
4 eggs, separated

50 g (2 oz) caster sugar
300 ml (10 fl oz) whipping cream
5 ml (1 tsp) vanilla essence

1 Preheat the grill to medium hot.

2 Combine the breadcrumbs with the demerara sugar and spread out on a baking tray. Place under the medium-hot grill and toast, stirring with a fork, until crunchy and brown. Watch carefully as the breadcrumbs burn quickly. Allow the browned crumbs to cool completely - they should be crispy in texture.

3 In a mixing bowl, whisk the egg whites to form stiff peaks. Add the sugar a little at a time, whisking after each addition, until stiff. Whisk in the egg yolks.

4 In a separate bowl, whip the cream with the vanilla essence until the same consistency as the egg mixture. Add the browned crumbs to the cream, then combine with the egg mixture. Transfer to a large freezerproof container, cover and freeze for at least 4 hours until firm.

5 Allow the ice-cream to stand at room temperature for about 5 minutes, to soften slightly, before serving.

NUTRITIONAL INFORMATION (PER SERVING)
Energy 680 kJ/206 kcal ■ Protein 4 g ■ Carbohydrate 17 g ■ Fat 14 g

BRANDYSNAP BASKETS WITH REDCURRANT SORBET

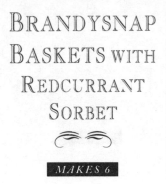

MAKES 6

AN ELEGANT END to a meal for a special occasion, the tangy freshness of the redcurrant sorbet perfectly complements the sweetness and texture of the brandy snap baskets. Ingeniously, the baskets are made by draping the cooked brandy-snap mixture over oiled oranges.

If redcurrants are not in season, substitute with summer berries as available.

INGREDIENTS

40 g (1 1/2 oz) margarine
15 ml (1 tbs) golden syrup
7.5 ml (1/2 tbs) lemon juice
50 g (2 oz) sugar

50 g (2 oz) Rite-Diet Flour Mix
5 ml (1 tsp) ground ginger
fresh mint leaves, to decorate

REDCURRANT SORBET

75 g (3 oz) sugar
110 ml (4 fl oz) water
450 g (1 lb) redcurrants

60 ml (4 tbs) white wine
15 ml (1 tbs) icing sugar
1 egg white

1 To make the redcurrant sorbet, heat the sugar and water in a small pan over low heat until the sugar has dissolved. Bring to the boil, then boil rapidly for 5 minutes, without stirring, to form a thick syrup. Allow to cool.

2 Place the redcurrants in a pan with the wine and icing sugar and cook gently for 15 minutes until the fruit is soft and juicy. Purée in a food processor or blender, then pass through a sieve to remove seeds and skin. Stir the syrup into the purée then pour into a freezerproof container. Freeze for about 1 1/2 hours until slushy.

3 Transfer the mixture to a large mixing bowl and whisk until smooth. In a separate bowl, whisk the egg white until stiff and fold in. Return to the freezing container and freeze for 2-3 hours until firm.

4 To make the brandysnap baskets, preheat the oven to 200°C/400°F/ Gas 6. Grease a baking sheet.

5 Melt the margarine and syrup in a pan. Add the lemon juice and sugar and stir well. Add the Flour Mix and ginger and beat well to mix. Drop 4 heaped teaspoons of the mixture onto the prepared baking sheet, spacing them well apart.

6 Bake in the oven for 6-8 minutes until the biscuits have spread and are golden. Allow to cool for 30 seconds, then remove from the baking sheet with a palette knife and drape over oiled oranges. Allow to cool before removing from the moulds. Make all the baskets in the same way.

7 Remove the sorbet from the freezer 15 minutes before serving to allow it to soften slightly. To serve, arrange a scoop of sorbet in each basket and decorate with mint leaves.

NUTRITIONAL INFORMATION (PER SERVING)
Energy 655 kJ/157 kcal ▪ _Protein 2 g_ ▪ _Carbohydrate 30 g_ ▪ _Fat 4 g_

PEARS IN SPICED WINE

SERVES 6

THIS REFRESHING FRUIT dish is an excellent way of using hard pears that refuse to soften up in the fruit bowl. The spiced wine gives a festive flavour that makes this dessert suitable for special occasions. The pan you use must be deep enough to allow the pears to stand upright.

INGREDIENTS

110 ml (4 fl oz) medium dry
white wine
110 ml (4 fl oz) water
110 g (4 oz) sugar
2.5 ml ($^1/_2$ tsp) ground cinnamon

4 whole cloves
pared rind and juice of $^1/_2$ lemon
6 dessert pears
toasted flaked almonds,
to decorate

1 Place the wine and water in a pan with the sugar, cinnamon, cloves and lemon rind and juice. Bring to the boil.

2 Peel the pears, leaving them whole and with the stalks on. Stand the pears upright in the pan. Pour the wine sauce over the pears, then cover the pan tightly and simmer gently for about 20 minutes until just tender. Remove with a slotted spoon and stand upright in a serving dish.

3 Boil the sauce rapidly for about 10 minutes until reduced by half to form a syrup and pour over the pears. Baste the pears with the syrup several times, then leave overnight in a cool place.

4 About 1 hour before serving, baste the pears again. Just before serving, sprinkle with the almonds.

NUTRITIONAL INFORMATION (PER SERVING)

Energy 315 kJ/75 kcal ■ *Protein (trace)* ■ *Carbohydrate 20 g* ■ *Fat (trace)*

SERVE THIS EXOTIC, yoghurt-based dessert with ratafia biscuits which are like small macaroons. They are readily available in most large supermarkets. Made from almonds and egg white, ratafia biscuits are wheat-free and make an excellent accompaniment to creamy desserts.

MANGO AND GINGER WHIP

SERVES 4

INGREDIENTS

2 large ripe mangoes	*300 ml (10 fl oz) Greek yoghurt*
3 pieces stem ginger in syrup, plus	*2 egg whites*
30 ml (2 tbs) syrup	*chopped stem ginger,*
juice of ½ orange	*to decorate*

1 To peel each mango, hold over a plate to catch the juices, and score the skin lengthways into sections using a small sharp knife. Holding the knife under the skin at one end of a section, pull the skin away from the flesh. Repeat with remaining sections. Slice large pieces of the flesh from the central stone. Scrape any remaining flesh from the skin and add to the slices with any juices.

2 Place the mango flesh and juices in a food processor or blender. Roughly chop the stem ginger and add to the mango with the ginger syrup and orange juice. Work until smooth. Fold in the yoghurt.

3 Whisk the egg whites until they stand in soft peaks. Using a large metal spoon, lightly stir a little of the whisked egg whites into the mango purée mixture, then fold in the remainder.

4 Spoon the whip into glasses and serve at one, decorated with stem ginger, or chill until ready to serve.

NUTRITIONAL INFORMATION (PER SERVING)
Energy 535 kJ/128 kcal ▪ Protein 6 g ▪ Carbohydrate 11 g ▪ Fat 7 g

FLAN JEANETTE

SERVES 8

A DELICIOUS VARIATION on Bakewell Tart, this irresistible flan is filled with apricots and an almond-flavoured sponge. Serve hot with fromage frais for a luscious dessert, or offer cold slices with coffee. For an attractive finish scatter the top of the flan with flaked almonds before baking.

INGREDIENTS

30 ml (2 tbs) apricot jam
400 g (14 oz) can apricot halves, drained
110 g (4 oz) caster sugar
110 g (4 oz) margarine
2 eggs

110 g (4 oz) Rite-Diet Flour Mix
5 ml (1 tsp) gluten-free baking powder
25 g (1 oz) ground almonds
icing sugar, for dusting

PASTRY

175 g (6 oz) Rite-Diet Flour Mix
75 g (3 oz) margarine

30 ml (2 tbs) water
1 egg

1 To make the pastry, put the Flour Mix and margarine in a mixing bowl and lightly rub together with your fingertips until the mixture resembles fine breadcrumbs. Add the water and egg and cut in with a knife. Bring together by hand to form a soft dough, then knead gently on a surface lightly floured with Flour Mix and roll out between two sheets of greaseproof paper. Transfer the pastry using the paper to an 18 cm (7 in) flan ring and gently press into place. Trim with a knife.

2 Preheat the oven to 180°C/350°F/Gas 4.

3 Spread the base of the pastry case with the jam and arrange the drained apricot halves on top. Cream together the sugar and margarine until light and fluffy, then gradually beat in the eggs. Carefully fold in the Flour Mix baking powder and ground almonds with a metal spoon. Spread the mixture over the apricots.

4 Bake the flan in the oven for about 40 minutes or until golden brown. Serve hot or cold, dusted with icing sugar.

NUTRITIONAL INFORMATION (PER SERVING)
Energy 1777 kJ/425 kcal ▪ Protein 6 g ▪ Carbohydrate 54 g ▪ Fat 22 g

MADE WITH A crushed biscuit base instead of the usual pastry case this family favourite is particularly quick and easy to make. Served cold, it provides a refreshing and not too filling end to a meal. Take care not to overbeat the egg whites. For an attractive finish, try piping the meringue topping over the lemon filling.

LEMON MERINGUE PIE

SERVES 6

INGREDIENTS

50 g (2 oz) butter
3 sachets Glutafin Digestive Biscuits
25 g (1 oz) Rite-Diet Flour Mix
grated rind and juice of 2 lemons

150 ml (5 fl oz) water
110 g (4 oz) sugar
2 eggs, separated

1 Melt the butter in a pan. Add the crushed biscuits and mix together. Turn the crumbs into an 18 cm (7 in) flan dish and press firmly to form a base.

2 Preheat the oven to 150°C/300°F/Gas 2.

3 Combine the Flour Mix, lemon rind and juice and water in a pan. Heat, stirring, until the mixture comes to the boil. Simmer for a few minutes, then remove from the heat. Add the egg yolks and 30 ml (2 tbs) sugar and stir well. Pour the lemon filling over the crumb base.

4 Whisk the egg whites until stiff. Whisk in half the sugar, then fold in the remaining sugar with a metal spoon. Spoon the meringue over the lemon filling and bake for 15-20 minutes until the peaks have browned. Allow to cool before serving.

NUTRITIONAL INFORMATION (PER SERVING)
Energy 724 kJ/174 kcal ▪ Protein 4 g ▪ Carbohydrate 13 g ▪ Fat 12 g

CAKES &
BISCUITS

VARY THE TASTE of this easy-to-make cake by using flavoured yoghurt, then decorate the cake with fruit to match the yoghurt flavour.

The time-saving feature of this cake is that the ingredients can be measured out with an empty 150 ml (5 fl oz) yoghurt pot! Use 3 pots Baking Mix, 1 pot yoghurt, 1/2 pot oil and 1 1/2 pots sugar.

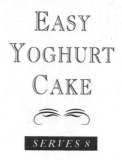

EASY YOGHURT CAKE

SERVES 8

INGREDIENTS

3 eggs, separated
225 g (8 oz) caster sugar
150 ml(5 fl oz) natural yoghurt

300 g (11 oz) Glutafin Baking Mix
75 ml (3 fl oz) vegetable oil

APRICOT GLAZE

25 g (1 oz) apricot jam
15 ml (1 tbs) flaked almonds

1 Preheat the oven to 180°C/375°F/Gas 5. Grease a deep 23 cm (9 in) round cake tin and line the base with greaseproof paper.

2 Whisk the egg yolks and sugar until thick and creamy. Whisk in the yoghurt. Add the Baking Mix and oil and stir in thoroughly.

3 In a separate bowl, whisk the egg whites until stiff and fold carefully into the mixture. Pour the mixture into the prepared cake tin and bake in the oven for 35-40 minutes until golden and springy to the touch.

4 To make the glaze, sieve the jam into a small pan and heat gently until melted. Brush the jam over the top of the cake and sprinkle with flaked almonds. Allow to cool before serving.

NUTRITIONAL INFORMATION (PER SERVING)
Energy 1610 kJ/385 kcal ▪ *Protein 7 g* ▪ *Carbohydrate 64 g* ▪ *Fat 13 g*

LEMON SYRUP CAKE

≈≈

SERVES 10

SOAKED IN A lemon syrup, this easy-to-make cake has a lovely tangy flavour and a mouthwateringly moist texture.

It is a prime example of what is so good about gluten-free cakes; so light you feel it may float away at any minute!

INGREDIENTS

225 g (8 oz) Glutafin
Baking Mix
110 g (4 oz) margarine
110 g (4 oz) caster sugar

5 ml (1 tsp) gluten-free
baking powder
2 eggs
finely grated rind of 1 lemon
icing sugar, for dusting

LEMON SYRUP

75 g (3 oz) icing sugar
juice of 1 large lemon

1 Preheat the oven to 180°C/350°F/Gas 4. Grease a 1.5 L (2½pt) loaf tin.

2 Place the Baking Mix, margarine, sugar, baking powder, egg and lemon rind in a mixing bowl and beat together by hand or with an electric mixer until light and fluffy and of a soft dropping consistency. Pour into the tin and level off with the back of a spoon.

3 Bake in the oven for about 45 minutes until firm and springy to the touch.

4 Meanwhile make the lemon syrup. Place the icing sugar and lemon juice in a small pan and heat gently until clear, stirring with a wooden spoon.

5 Pour the syrup over the hot cake while it is still in the tin. Leave to cool in the tin to allow the syrup to soak through. When completely cool, turn out onto a plate and dust with icing sugar.

NUTRITIONAL INFORMATION (PER SERVING)
Energy 1010 kJ/241 kcal ■ Protein 3 g ■ Carbohydrate 37 g ■ Fat 10 g

THIS ATTRACTIVE CAKE has a continental flavour and, like all cakes made without wheatflour, is deliciously light and moist. If preferred, it could also be made in a loaf tin and covered with melted plain chocolate instead of icing sugar.

MARBLE CAKE

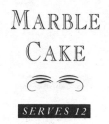

SERVES 12

INGREDIENTS

110 g (4 oz) Rite-Diet Flour Mix
5 ml (1 tsp) gluten-free
baking powder
110 g (4 oz) margarine
110 g (4 oz) caster sugar
2 eggs, beaten

2.5 ml (¹/₂ tsp) vanilla essence
15 ml (1 tbs) gluten-free cocoa
powder, dissolved in 30 ml (2 tbs)
hot water and cooled
icing sugar, for dusting

1 Preheat the oven to 180°C/350°F/Gas 4. Grease an 18 cm (7 in) ring cake mould.

2 Place the Flour Mix, baking powder, margarine, sugar, eggs and vanilla essence in a mixing bowl. Beat together for about 2 minutes with an electric mixer or by hand for a few minutes until the mixture is creamy and of a soft dropping consistency.

3 Remove one third of the cake mixture and beat the cocoa mixture into it.

4 Spoon the vanilla-flavoured mixture into the prepared mould, then spoon the cocoa-flavoured mixture on top. Using a knife, cut and turn the two mixtures to form ripples.

5 Bake in the oven for 40-45 minutes until golden and springy to the touch. Leave in the tin for 5 minutes before turning out onto a wire rack. Allow to cool. Dust with icing sugar to serve.

NUTRITIONAL INFORMATION (PER SERVING)
Energy 640 kJ/153 kcal ■ *Protein 2 g* ■ *Carbohydrate 17 g* ■ *Fat 9 g*

ANGEL CAKE

SERVES 8

MADE WITH EGG whites, this American-style cake has a very distinctive texture. To ring the changes, sandwich the cake together with red-fruit conserve and dredge the top with icing sugar.

INGREDIENTS

3 egg whites

1.5 ml ($^1/4$ tsp) cream of tartar

50 g (2 oz) Glutafin Baking Mix

75 g (3 oz) caster sugar

2.5 ml ($^1/2$ tsp) vanilla essence

45 ml (3 tbs) wheat-free lemon curd

ICING

7.5 ml ($^1/2$ tbs) lemon juice

7.5 ml ($^1/2$ tbs) water

110 g (4 oz) icing sugar, sifted

1 Preheat the oven to 170°C/325°F/Gas 3.

2 In a mixing bowl, whisk the egg white until foaming. Add the cream of tartar and whisk until stiff peaks are formed. Carefully fold in the Baking Mix and sugar, about 30 ml (2 tbs) at a time, then fold in the vanilla essence. Pour the mixture into an ungreased 18 cm (7 in) ring cake tin (preferably an angel cake tin).

3 Bake the cake in the oven for 40-45 minutes until a skewer inserted into the cake comes out clean. Leave to cool in the tin for a few minutes before turning out. Slice the cake in half and sandwich back together with lemon curd.

4 To make the icing, beat the lemon juice and water into the icing sugar, then pour over the cake.

NUTRITIONAL INFORMATION (PER SERVING)

Energy 555 kJ/133 kcal ■ Protein 1 g ■ Carbohydrate 32 g ■ Fat 1 g

THIS CAKE IMPROVES in texture and flavour with keeping - store in an airtight tin or wrapped in cling film.

It can be eaten on its own or spread with butter, if preferred.

GINGERBREAD

SERVES 10

INGREDIENTS

75 g (3 oz) margarine
30 ml (2 tbs) golden syrup
30 ml (2 tbs) black treacle
75 g (3 oz) soft brown sugar
175 g (6 oz) Glutafin Baking Mix

5 ml (1 tsp) gluten-free baking powder
25 g (1 oz) wheat-free fibre or bran
10 ml (2 tsp) ground ginger
1 egg, beaten
150 ml (5 fl oz) milk

1 Preheat the oven to 180°C/350°F/Gas 4. Grease a 850 ml (1 1/2 lb) loaf tin.

2 Place the margarine, syrup, treacle and sugar in a pan and heat gently until the ingredients have melted. Combine the Baking Mix, baking powder, fibre and ginger in a mixing bowl. Add the egg, milk and melted mixture. Stir well to form a smooth pouring batter.

3 Pour the mixture into the prepared tin and bake in the oven for about 50-55 minutes until springy to the touch. Leave in the tin for a few minutes before turning out onto a wire rack. Slice when cold.

NUTRITIONAL INFORMATION (PER SERVING)
Energy 675 kJ/161 kcal ■ Protein 3 g ■ Carbohydrate 23 g ■ Fat 7 g

FARMHOUSE FRUIT CAKE

SERVES 12

A FIBRE-RICH cake, ideal to serve with mid-morning coffee or as a tea-time treat. Store in an airtight tin to keep it fresh and moist.

This recipe is one you can rely on – it has been tried and tested to ensure that whatever happens, the fruit will not sink to the bottom!

INGREDIENTS

225 g (8 oz) Glutafin Baking Mix	75 g (3 oz) soft brown sugar
25 g (1 oz) wheat-free fibre or bran	150 g (5 oz) sultanas
10 ml (2 tsp) gluten-free baking powder	50 g (2 oz) mixed peel
5 ml (1 tsp) grated nutmeg	50 g (2 oz) glacé cherries
75 g (3 oz) margarine	juice of ¹/2 lemon
	150 ml (5 fl oz) milk
	2 eggs

1 Preheat the oven to 180°C/350°F/Gas 4. Grease and line a deep 19 cm (7 ¹/2 in) round cake tin or an 850 ml (1 ¹/2 pt) loaf tin.

2 Place the Baking Mix, fibre, baking powder, nutmeg, margarine and brown sugar in a mixing bowl and stir well. Add the fruit, lemon juice, milk and eggs, then beat until a smooth light batter is formed.

3 Pour the cake batter into the prepared tin and bake for 1 hour until golden brown and firm to the touch. Remove from the tin and cool on a wire rack.

NUTRITIONAL INFORMATION (PER SERVING)
Energy 850 kJ/203 kcal ■ Protein 3 g ■ Carbohydrate 34 g ■ Fat 7 g

DO NOT BE put off by the idea of using carrots in a cake - their use ensures that the finished product is not only very moist, sweet and delicious, but good for you too!

As a variation, flavour the cake mixture with grated orange rind and use orange rind and juice in the topping instead of lemon.

CARROT AND HAZELNUT CAKE

SERVES 8

INGREDIENTS

3 eggs, separated
110 g (4 oz) sugar
225 g (8 oz) carrots, grated
110 g (4 oz) hazelnuts, ground
finely grated rind of 1 lemon

75 g (3 oz) Rite-Diet Flour Mix
or 50 g (2 oz) rice flour
5 ml (1 tsp) gluten-free
baking powder

TOPPING

75 g (3 oz) curd cheese
15 ml (1 tbs) fromage frais
15 ml (1 tbs) icing sugar

10 ml (2 tsp) finely grated
lemon rind
10 ml (2 tsp) lemon juice

1 Preheat the oven to 180°C/350°F/Gas 4. Grease a deep 15 cm (6 in) round tin, preferably loose bottomed, and line the base with greaseproof paper.

2 In a bowl, whisk the egg yolks and sugar together until thick and creamy. Add the grated carrots, ground hazelnuts, lemon rind, Flour Mix and baking powder and stir to blend well. In a separate bowl, whisk the egg whites until stiff and gently fold in.

3 Pour the cake mixture into the prepared tin and bake in the oven for about 40 minutes until a warmed skewer inserted into the centre comes out clean. Leave in the tin for a few minutes before turning out. Cool on a wire rack.

4 To make the topping, beat the curd cheese with the fromage frais, icing sugar and lemon rind and juice, then spread over the top of the cold cake.

NUTRITIONAL INFORMATION (PER SERVING)
Energy 890 kJ/213 kcal ▪ Protein 5 g ▪ Carbohydrate 25 g ▪ Fat 11 g

BLACK FOREST GATEAU

SERVES 10

THIS IS A REALLY special treat for anyone on a wheat-free diet, and need no longer be on the 'forbidden' list.

A ready-made wheat-free black cherry pie filling can be used instead of canned cherries, if wished.

INGREDIENTS

350 g (12 oz) Glutafin Baking Mix
175 g (6 oz) caster sugar
7.5 ml (1 1/2 tsp) gluten-free baking powder
175 g (6 oz) margarine

3 eggs
15 ml (1 tbs) gluten-free cocoa powder, dissolved in 15 ml (1 tbs) hot water and cooled

FILLING AND DECORATION

400 g (14 oz) can black cherries in syrup, pitted
15 ml (1 tbs) arrowroot
10 ml (2 tsp) Kirsch (optional)

600 ml (1 pt) whipping cream
60 ml (4 tbs) cherry jam
150 g (5 oz) dark chocolate, grated

1 Preheat the oven to 180°C/350°F/Gas 4. Grease two 20 cm (8 in) sandwich tins and line the bases with greaseproof paper.

2 Place the Baking Mix, sugar, baking powder, margarine and eggs in a mixing bowl. Beat together with an electric mixer for about 2 minutes or beat by hand for 5 minutes until the mixture is creamy and of a soft dropping consistency. Beat in the cocoa mixture and divide between the prepared tins.

3 Bake the cakes in the oven for about 25-30 minutes until golden and springy to the touch. Turn out and cool on a wire rack.

4 To make the filling, drain the cherries and make up the syrup to 250 ml (9 fl oz) with water. Place 25 ml (1 fl oz) of the liquid in a small pan, add the arrowroot and mix to a paste. Add the rest of the liquid and heat slowly, stirring continuously, until a thick sauce is formed. Add the Kirsch, if using, and leave to cool. Add most of the pitted cherries, reserving some for decoration.

5 Split each cake into two layers with a sharp knife. Whip the cream until stiff and sandwich the cakes together by spreading the first layer with jam and the cherry sauce, the second layer with cream, and the third layer with jam and sauce.

6 Spread cream over the top and sides of the cake, then coat the sides with grated chocolate. Finish with whirls of piped cream and decorate the top with the reserved cherries and a generous sprinkling of grated chocolate.

NUTRITIONAL INFORMATION (PER SERVING)
Energy 2767 kJ/667 kcal ■ Protein 6 g ■ Carbohydrate 65 g ■ Fat 44 g

MANDARIN AND CREAM ROLL

SERVES 8

THIS LUSCIOUS CREAM-FILLED Swiss roll sponge is a real treat! For a special occasion fill the roll with strawberries and flavour the cream with a little orange liqueur.

To make a chocolate sponge, replace 15 g (1/2 oz) Glutafin Baking Mix with the same quantity of gluten-free cocoa powder.

INGREDIENTS

3 eggs

75 g (3 oz) caster sugar

2-3 drops vanilla essence

75 g (3 oz) Glutafin Baking Mix

FILLING

300 ml (10 fl oz) whipping cream

300 g (11 oz) can mandarin oranges, drained

25 g (1 oz) dark chocolate

2 glacé cherries

icing sugar, for dusting

1 Preheat the oven to 200°C/400°F/Gas 6. Grease and line a 25 x 30 cm (10 x 12 in) rectangular Swiss roll tin.

2 In a bowl, whisk the eggs and sugar until thick and fluffy and the mixture leaves a trail when the whisk is lifted. Add the vanilla essence. Gently fold in the Baking Mix with a metal spoon and pour the mixture into the prepared tin. Bake for 10-15 minutes until golden brown and the sponge springs back when lightly pressed.

3 Immediately turn out onto a sheet of greaseproof paper which has been sprinkled with caster sugar. Neaten the edges with a sharp knife and roll up from the shorter side. Leave to cool.

4 Meanwhile, whip the cream until firm. Chop one third of the mandarins and place in a bowl, then stir in three-quarters of the cream.

5 Unroll the cold sponge and spread with the mandarin cream. Re-roll. Dust with icing sugar and pipe the remaining cream along the centre of the Swiss roll. Decorate with the remaining mandarins and cherries.

NUTRITIONAL INFORMATION (PER SERVING)
Energy 1260 kJ/301 kcal ■ Protein 5 g ■ Carbohydrate 32 g ■ Fat 17 g

PACKED WITH FIBRE, this easy-to-make fruit cake has a delicious texture and features an unusual crunchy topping. Ideal as a healthy addition to a lunch box, it is also excellent served as a tea-time treat.

MUESLI CAKE

SERVES 10

INGREDIENTS

175 g (6 oz) Rite-Diet Flour Mix
10 ml (2 tsp) gluten-free
baking powder
75 g (3 oz) soft brown sugar
50 g (2 oz) gluten-free muesli
50 g (2 oz) Rite-Diet Hot Breakfast
Cereal or buckwheat flakes

200 ml (7 fl oz) milk
1 egg, beaten
50 g (2 oz) sultanas
25 g (1 oz) margarine, melted
1.5 ml ($^1/4$ tsp) ground cinnamon
1 cooking apple, thinly sliced

TOPPING

50 g (2 oz) Rite-Diet Hot Breakfast
Cereal or buckwheat flakes
50 g (2 oz) soft brown sugar

50 g (2 oz) sultanas
50 g (2 oz) Rite-Diet Flour Mix
75 g (3 oz) margarine, melted

1 Preheat the oven to 180°C/350°F/Gas 4.

2 Place the Flour Mix, baking powder, sugar, muesli and Breakfast Cereal in a mixing bowl and stir well together. Add the milk, egg, sultanas, margarine and cinnamon and beat well. Spoon into a loose bottomed 18 cm (7 in) non-stick round cake tin and cover with apple slices.

3 To make the topping combine the Breakfast Cereal with the sugar, sultanas, Flour Mix and margarine. Sprinkle over the apples and bake in the oven for about 45-50 minutes until cooked through. Leave to cool before removing from the tin.

NUTRITIONAL INFORMATION (PER SERVING)
Energy 1345 kJ/319 kcal ▪ Protein 5 g ▪ Carbohydrate 53 g ▪ Fat 11 g

COFFEE AND WALNUT GATEAU

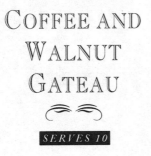

SERVES 10

DECORATED AND FILLED with a luscious coffee-flavoured buttercream, this more sophisticated alternative to Black Forest Gateau is hard to resist with a cup of strong coffee when it's time for elevenses. The texture of the sponge is improved if it is wrapped in cling film and stored for a day before decorating with buttercream.

INGREDIENTS

350 g (12 oz) Glutafin
Baking Mix
175 g (6 oz) caster sugar
7.5 ml (1 1/2 tsp) gluten-free
baking powder
175 g (6 oz) soft margarine
3 eggs

7.5 ml (1 1/2 tsp) instant coffee,
dissolved in
15 ml (1 tbs) hot water and cooled
110 g (4 oz) walnuts, finely chopped,
for coating
walnuts halves and sugar coffee
beans, to decorate

COFFEE BUTTERCREAM

110 g (4 oz) butter
250 g (9 oz) icing sugar, sifted
7.5 ml (1 1/2 tsp) instant coffee, dissolved in
15 ml (1 tbs) hot water
and cooled

1 Preheat the oven to 180°C/350°F/Gas 4. Grease 2 deep 20 cm (8 in) round cake tins and line the bases with greaseproof paper.

2 Place the Baking Mix, sugar, baking powder, margarine and eggs in a mixing bowl. Beat together for about 2 minutes with an electric mixer, or by hand for 5 minutes until the mixture is creamy and of a soft dropping consistency. Beat in the coffee mixture and divide between the prepared tins.

3 Bake the cakes in the oven for 25-30 minutes until golden and springy to the touch. Turn out and cool on a wire rack.

4 To make the coffee buttercream, cream the butter in a bowl, then gradually beat in all the icing sugar. Beat in the coffee mixture.

5 Sandwich the cakes together with a third of the buttercream. Spread a thin layer of buttercream over the sides, then roll in the chopped nuts to coat evenly. Cover the top of the cake and finish by piping whirls of buttercream around the edge. Decorate with walnut halves and sugar coffee beans, transfer to a serving plate and chill until ready to serve.

NUTRITIONAL INFORMATION (PER SERVING)
Energy 2415 kJ/577 kcal ■ *Protein 6 g* ■ *Carbohydrate 73 g* ■ *Fat 31 g*

FLAPJACKS

MAKES 12

BUCKWHEAT FLAKES ARE used instead of the usual rolled oats to make flapjacks that anyone on a wheat-free diet can enjoy without worry. They are handy to slip into a school lunchbox.

INGREDIENTS

175 g (6 oz) margarine
30 ml (2 tbs) golden syrup
25 g (1 oz) wheat-free fibre or bran

175 g (6 oz) Rite-Diet Hot Breakfast Cereal or buckwheat flakes
110 g (4 oz) soft brown sugar

1 Preheat the oven to 180°C/350°F/Gas 4. Grease a 20 cm (8 in) square baking tin.

2 Melt the margarine in a large pan and add the syrup. Remove from the heat and stir in the remaining ingredients. Turn the mixture into the prepared tin and spread evenly with a spatula.

3 Bake in the oven for 20 minutes until golden brown. Cut into fingers while still warm. Cool and store in an airtight container.

NUTRITIONAL INFORMATION (PER SERVING)
Energy 885 kJ/211 kcal ■ Protein 2 g ■ Carbohydrate 23 g ■ Fat 13 g

MADE ENTIRELY WITHOUT flour, these elegant biscuits will add a touch of style to the tea-table.

If wished, the mixture can be piped through a star-shaped nozzle.

MACAROONS

MAKES 18

INGREDIENTS

175 g (6 oz) ground almonds
175 g (6 oz) caster sugar
2-3 drops vanilla essence

2 egg whites
blanched almonds, to decorate
caster sugar, for sprinkling

1 Preheat the oven to 180°C/350°F/Gas 4. Line 2 large baking trays with rice paper or non-stick parchment.

2 Mix the ground almonds and caster sugar together in a mixing bowl, then stir in the vanilla essence. Lightly beat the egg whites, then gradually stir into the almond mixture, adding enough to give a fairly stiff consistency - the mixture should be firm enough to hold its shape.

3 Place heaped tablespoons of the mixture onto the prepared baking trays, spacing them well apart to allow for spreading. Place an almond in the centre of each and sprinkle lightly with caster sugar.

4 Bake in the oven for about 15 minutes until firm and lightly coloured. Leave to cool on the trays for 2 minutes, then transfer to wire racks. When cold, remove the excess rice paper from the biscuits and serve.

NUTRITIONAL INFORMATION (PER SERVING)
Energy 508 kJ/121 kcal ■ Protein 3 g ■ Carbohydrate 13 g ■ Fat 7 g

CRUNCHY SLICES

MAKES 24

TASTE AND TEXTURE are the key words with these scrumptious chewy bars. The combination of coconut and cherries will keep adults and children alike coming back for more. Try smothering them in melted chocolate for an even-more 'sinful' treat.

INGREDIENTS

110 g (4 oz) margarine
60 ml (4 tbs) golden syrup
150 g (5 oz) desiccated coconut
50 g (2 oz) rice crispies or
gluten-free muesli

50 g (2 oz) glacé cherries
50 g (2 oz) ground almonds
50 g (2 oz) potato flour
2 eggs, lightly beaten

1 Preheat the oven to 180°C/350°F/Gas 4. Grease an 18 x 30 cm (8 x 12 in) Swiss roll tin.

2 Melt the margarine and golden syrup in a small saucepan over gentle heat. Combine the coconut, rice crispies, cherries, ground almonds and potato flour in a mixing bowl. Make a well in the middle, add the eggs and the melted mixture and stir well to blend.

3 Smooth the mixture into the prepared Swiss roll tin and bake in the oven for 20 minutes until golden brown. Cut into squares while hot and leave to cool in the tin.

NUTRITIONAL INFORMATION (PER SERVING)
Energy 315 kJ/75 kcal ▪ Protein 1 g ▪ Carbohydrate 7 g ▪ Fat 5 g

PERFECT FOR SLIPPING into a child's lunchbox as a special treat, these delicious biscuits are high in fibre and make an energy-filled snack. In fact, they are so easy to make that older children may like to have a go at making them themselves. When the biscuits have cooled down, store them in an airtight container and keep them hidden well away from little fingers!

CHOCOLATE, DATE AND NUT DELIGHTS

MAKES 18

INGREDIENTS

2 egg whites
110 g (4oz) caster sugar
50 g (2 oz) chopped walnuts
50 g (2 oz) chopped dried dates

50 g (2 oz) desiccated coconut
50 g (2 oz) chocolate chips or grated dark chocolate

1 Preheat the oven to 180°C/350°F/Gas 4. Grease and line 2 baking trays.

2 Whisk the egg whites until they form stiff peaks. Gradually add the sugar, a tablespoon at a time, whisking after each addition. Fold in the remaining ingredients and place small mounds of the mixture on the prepared trays, spacing them well apart.

3 Bake in the oven for 10 minutes until fairly crisp. Leave on the trays for a few minutes, then transfer to a wire rack to cool.

NUTRITIONAL INFORMATION (PER SERVING)
Energy 325 kJ/78 kcal ■ *Protein 1 g* ■ *Carbohydrate 10 g* ■ *Fat 4 g*

CAPTIONS FOR
THE FOLLOWING
FIVE COLOUR PAGES

Page 1 *(opposite)*
Quick and Easy Pizzas *(page 57)*

Page 2 *(overleaf)*
Brandysnap Baskets
with Redcurrant Sorbet *(page 102)*

Page 3
French Fruit Flan *(page 86)*

Page 4-5
FROM LEFT TO RIGHT
Pitta Bread *(page 132)* with Falafel *(page 73)*
Southern-style Chicken *(page 71)*
Tangy Fish Salad *(page 78)*

CAPTIONS FOR
THE PRECEDING
THREE COLOUR PAGES

❧ ❧

Page 6
TOP Marble Cake *(page 111)*
BOTTOM Macaroons *(page 123)*

❧ ❧

Page 7
TOP Easy Yoghurt Cake *(page 109)*
CENTRE Carrot and Hazelnut Cake *(page 115)*
BOTTOM Lemon Syrup Cake *(page 110)*

❧ ❧

Page 8 *(opposite)*
TOP Mixed Grain Bread *(page 128)*
BOTTOM Tea Cakes *(page 134)*

PEANUT COOKIES

MAKES 25

THESE CRUNCHY BISCUITS are easy to make and will be popular with all the family. Give the cookies an attractive crisscross pattern by pressing the dough twice with the prongs of the fork, the second time holding the fork at right angles to the first indentations.

INGREDIENTS

110 g (4 oz) margarine
110 g (4 oz) caster sugar
1 egg
225 g (8 oz) Glutafin Baking Mix
2.5 ml (1/2 tsp) bicarbonate of soda

2.5 ml (1/2 tsp) gluten-free baking powder
110 g (4 oz) salted peanuts
75 g (3 oz) cornflakes
75 g (3 oz) Rite-Diet Hot Breakfast Cereal or buckwheat flakes

1 Preheat the oven to 180°C/350°F/Gas 4. Grease 2 baking trays.

2 In a mixing bowl, cream the margarine and sugar together until light and fluffy. Gradually beat in the egg, then mix in the Baking Mix, bicarbonate of soda and baking powder. Add the remaining ingredients and work into a soft dough.

3 Divide the dough into 25 even-sized pieces and roll each piece into a ball. Place on the prepared baking trays, spacing them well apart. Flatten each ball with a fork as described above.

4 Bake the biscuits for 10 minutes until golden brown. Using a palette knife, immediately loosen the biscuits from the tray and allow to cool before transferring to a wire rack. When cold, store in an airtight container.

NUTRITIONAL INFORMATION (PER SERVING)
Energy 525 kJ/126 kcal ■ *Protein 2 g* ■ *Carbohydrate 17 g* ■ *Fat 6 g*

BREAD & BUNS

MIXED GRAIN BREAD

MAKES 2 LOAVES

THE NUTRITIOUS VALUE of seeds and grains is second to none, and they give this loaf a wonderful texture and flavour. Made fresh every week, this country-style loaf could become the mainstay of your everyday diet.

INGREDIENTS

50 g (2 oz) wheat-free fibre or bran
450 ml (15 fl oz) tepid water
500 g (1 lb) Glutafin Baking Mix
10 g (1 sachet) dried yeast
15 ml (1 tbs) sunflower seeds
15 ml (1 tbs) sesame seeds
15 ml (1 tbs) linseed

15 ml (1 tbs) buckwheat flakes
15 ml (1 tbs) roasted whole buckwheat
5 ml (1 tsp) salt
30 ml (2 tbs) vegetable oil
milk, to glaze
5 ml (1 tsp) sesame seeds

1 Grease two non-stick 1 L (2 pt) loaf tins.

2 Soak the fibre in half the measured water and leave to stand for 10 minutes.

3 Place the Baking Mix, yeast, mixed seeds, buckwheat and salt into a mixing bowl and stir. Add the remaining tepid water, soaked fibre and oil. Beat for 2 minutes in an electric mixer on slow speed. Scrape down the bowl and beat for a further 2 minutes on medium speed to give a smooth thick batter. Alternatively, beat the ingredients together with a wooden spoon for 5 minutes.

4 Divide the batter between the prepared loaf tins. Cover with a polythene bag and leave the dough to rise in a warm place for about 30 minutes, until doubled in size.

5 Meanwhile, preheat the oven to 220°C/425°F/Gas 7.

6 Brush the risen dough with milk and sprinkle with sesame seeds. Bake in the oven for about 25 minutes until the loaves are golden and firm. Remove from the tins and cool on a wire rack.

NUTRITIONAL INFORMATION (PER SERVING)
Energy 430 kJ/103 kcal ■ Protein 2 g ■ Carbohydrate 18 g ■ Fat 3 g

USE THIS WHEAT-FREE recipe to make 10 baps - divide the uncooked batter between 10 greased bap tins, rise and glaze as described, then bake for 10-15 minutes.

To add extra flavour to the bread, sprinkle the glazed batter with poppy seeds.

BASIC WHITE BREAD

MAKES 2 LOAVES

INGREDIENTS

500 g (1 lb) Glutafin Baking Mix
2.5 ml (1/2 tsp) salt
10 g (1 sachet) dried yeast

320 ml (11 fl oz) tepid water
30 ml (2 tbs) vegetable oil
beaten egg or vegetable oil, to glaze

1 Grease 2 non-stick 1 L (2 pt) loaf tins. Place the Baking Mix, salt and yeast in a mixing bowl and stir. Add the tepid water and oil. Beat for 2 minutes in an electric mixer on slow speed. Scrape down the bowl and beat for a further 2 minutes on medium speed to give a smooth thick batter. Alternatively, beat the ingredients together with a wooden spoon for 5 minutes.

2 Divide the batter between the prepared loaf tins. Cover with a polythene bag and leave the dough to rise in a warm place for about 30 minutes, or until doubled in size.

3 Meanwhile, preheat the oven to 220°C/425°F/Gas 7.

4 Brush the risen dough with beaten egg for a golden crust, or with oil for a smooth shiny top. Bake in the oven for about 25 minutes until the loaves are golden and firm. Remove from the tins and cool on a wire rack. Store in a polythene bag.

NUTRITIONAL INFORMATION (PER SERVING)
Energy 320 kJ/77 kcal ▪ *Protein 1 g* ▪ *Carbohydrate 17 g* ▪ *Fat 1 g*

CORNMEAL MUFFINS

MAKES 12

AN AMERICAN SPECIALITY, cornmeal muffins are traditionally served as a savoury snack. Cornmeal, often sold under its Italian name of Polenta, is made from ground sweetcorn. It has a coarse texture and sweetish flavour.

INGREDIENTS

110 g (4 oz) cornmeal
175 g (6 oz) Glutafin Baking Mix
50 g (2 oz) caster sugar
10 ml (2 tsp) gluten-free baking powder

5 ml (1 tsp) salt
1 large egg, beaten
250 ml (8 fl oz) milk
50 g (2 oz) margarine, melted

1 Preheat the oven to 200°C/400°F/Gas 6. Line 12 muffin tins or patty tins with muffin paper cones.

2 Place the cornmeal, Baking Mix, sugar, baking powder and salt in a large mixing bowl. Stir and make a well in the centre. Combine the egg, milk and melted margarine and pour into the well. Whisk together with a balloon whisk. Spoon the mixture into the prepared tins, filling them two-thirds full.

3 Bake in the oven for 20-25 minutes until golden and risen. Allow to cool slightly in the tins, then turn out onto a wire rack. Serve warm.

NUTRITIONAL INFORMATION (PER SERVING)
Energy 805 kJ/192 kcal ■ Protein 4 g ■ Carbohydrate 30 g ■ Fat 7 g

THIS UNUSUAL BREAD would make a good accompaniment to salad and is delicious served warm with matured Cheddar cheese and chutney.

For a walnut and olive loaf, replace the onion with 15 ml (1 tbs) finely chopped walnuts, replace the cumin with 15 ml (1 tbs) chopped black olives and use olive oil.

ONION AND CARAWAY SEED LOAF

MAKES 1 LOAF

INGREDIENTS

22.5 ml (1 1/2 tbs) vegetable oil
1/2 onion, finely chopped
250 g (9 oz) Rite-Diet Brown Bread Mix

5 ml (1 tsp) cumin seeds
5 ml (1 tsp) caraway seeds
5 g (1/2 sachet) dried yeast
225 ml (8 fl oz) tepid water

1 Grease a 1 L (2 pt) loaf tin. Heat 7.5 ml (1/2 tbs) oil in a pan, add the onion and cook gently for 5 minutes until softened.

2 Place the Baking Mix, cumin, caraway seeds and yeast in a mixing bowl. Add the water and remaining oil and mix to form a smooth batter. Add the lightly-fried onion and mix in well.

3 Place the dough in the prepared loaf tin and cover with a polythene bag. Leave to rise in a warm place for 30 minutes or until doubled in size.

4 Preheat the oven to 450°C/225°F/Gas 8.

5 Brush the top of the loaf with oil and bake in the oven for about 25 minutes until golden and firm.

NUTRITIONAL INFORMATION (PER SERVING)
Energy 300 kJ/72 kcal ■ Protein 1 g ■ Carbohydrate 3 g ■ Fat 11 g

PITTA BREAD

MAKES 4

THE TRADITIONAL ACCOMPANIMENT to Taramasalata and other Greek dips, pitta bread is popular with adults and children alike. For a healthy packed lunch, split open a pitta and fill with falafel and salad.

INGREDIENTS

225 g (8 oz) Rite-Diet Flour Mix
2.5 ml (1/2 tsp) dried yeast

175 ml (6 fl oz) tepid water
15 ml (1 tbs) vegetable oil

1 Preheat the oven to 230°C/450°F/Gas 8. Grease 2 baking trays.

2 Place the Flour Mix and yeast in a mixing bowl and stir. Add the tepid water and oil and beat together with a wooden spoon for 5 minutes to form a smooth, kneadable dough. Alternatively, beat the ingredients together with an electric mixer on slow speed for 2 minutes to form a dough. Knead well.

3 Divide the dough into 4 pieces and roll out on a surface lightly floured with Flour Mix to make oval shapes, about 20 cm (8 in) long and 10 cm (4 in) wide. Transfer to one of the prepared baking trays, cover with oiled polythene and leave in a warm place for 15 minutes to rise.

4 Meanwhile, place the other baking tray in the oven to heat up.

5 Transfer the dough to the hot tray and bake in the oven for 10 minutes until risen, puffed and golden brown. Cool and serve.

NUTRITIONAL INFORMATION (PER SERVING)
Energy 940 kJ/225 kcal ■ Protein 5 g ■ Carbohydrate 45 g ■ Fat 4 g

THIS DELICIOUS TEABREAD is moist enough to serve on its own, simply cut into slices. Alternatively, it can be buttered and slipped into lunch boxes or as part of a wholesome tea. Children simply love it at any time of day.

BANANA BREAD

MAKES 10 SLICES

INGREDIENTS

1 large ripe banana
1 egg
110 g (4 oz) sugar
50 g (2 oz) margarine

2.5 ml (¹/2 tsp) vanilla essence
150 g (5 oz) Rite-Diet Flour Mix
1.5 ml (¹/4 tsp) salt
1.5 ml (¹/4 tsp) bicarbonate of soda

1 Preheat the oven to 190°C/375°F/Gas 5. Grease a non-stick 1 L (2 pt) loaf tin.

2 In a bowl, beat the banana with the egg, sugar, margarine and vanilla essence until smooth. In a separate bowl, combine the Flour Mix with the salt and bicarbonate of soda, then add the banana mixture and stir well.

3 Pour the mixture into the prepared tin and bake in the oven for about 40 minutes until golden and firm. Turn out and leave to cool on a wire rack.

NUTRITIONAL INFORMATION (PER SERVING)
Energy 615 kJ/147 kcal ▪ Protein 2 g ▪ Carbohydrate 25 g ▪ Fat 5 g

TEA CAKES

MAKES 8

THE AGONIZING DAYS of watching other people tucking into forbidden tea-time favourites are now over! These wheat-free tea cakes are just as good as the old-fashioned version!

INGREDIENTS

275 g (10 oz) Rite-Diet White
Bread Mix
2.5 ml (1/2 tsp) ground cinnamon
2.5 ml (1/2 tsp) grated nutmeg
25 g (1 oz) sugar
25 g (1 oz) butter, melted

1/2 egg, beaten
75 ml (3 fl oz) milk
45 ml (3 tbs) water
50 g (2 oz) currants
15 g (1/2 oz) chopped mixed peel

GLAZE

5 ml (1 tsp) milk
5 ml (1 tsp) water
25 g (1 oz) caster sugar

1 Preheat the oven to 190°C/375°F/Gas 5. Grease a baking tray.

2 Sift the Bread Mix and spices into a mixing bowl, then stir in the sugar. Make a well in the centre and add the melted butter, egg, milk and water. Bring together to form a dough. Add the currants and mixed peel and knead in.

3 Transfer the dough to a surface lightly floured with Bread Mix and knead until smooth. Divide into 8 portions and shape into buns. Place the buns on the prepared baking tray and bake in the oven for about 20 minutes until golden brown.

4 Meanwhile, mix together the ingredients for the glaze.

5 Remove the buns from the oven and immediately brush with the sugar glaze. Cool before serving.

NUTRITIONAL INFORMATION (PER SERVING)
Energy 825 kJ/196 kcal ■ Protein 3 g ■ Carbohydrate 38 g ■ Fat 4 g

FOR SAVOURY CHEESE scones, omit the sugar and dried fruit and add 75 g (3 oz) grated Cheddar cheese.

Split each scone in half and top with whipped cream or fromage frais and fresh strawberries for a truly indulgent country-style cream tea.

TRADITIONAL SCONES

MAKES 8

INGREDIENTS

225 g (8 oz) Glutafin
Baking Mix
large pinch of salt
50 g (2 oz) butter
or margarine

25 g (1 oz) sugar
50 g (2 oz) dried fruit
75 ml (3 fl oz) milk
or beaten egg, to glaze

1 Preheat the oven to 220°C/425°F/Gas 7. Grease a baking tray.

2 Place the Baking Mix and salt in a mixing bowl. Rub in the butter until the mixture resembles breadcrumbs. Add the sugar and dried fruit and stir. Add the milk and bring together to form a soft dough. Knead lightly until smooth.

3 Roll out or press to a thickness of 2 cm (3/4 in). Using a 5 cm (2 in) round cutter, cut out rounds. Alternatively, shape the dough into a round and mark into triangles. Brush with milk or egg to glaze.

4 Place on the prepared baking tray and bake in the oven for 10-12 minutes or until golden brown and well risen. Cool before serving.

NUTRITIONAL INFORMATION (PER SERVING)
Energy 142 kJ/34 kcal ■ *Protein 1 g* ■ *Carbohydrate 13 g* ■ *Fat 0.5 g*

INDEX

AUTHOR'S ACKNOWLEDGEMENT

I would like to thank several people who have helped to bring this book to publication.

Firstly, Angela Dibble for her practical contribution and dedication in testing and retesting all the recipes, Tali Goldman for her help and support, Dr Geraldine Fitzgerald for nutritional advice, Joanne Lloyd and Elizabeth Mayes for preparing nutritional analysis.

Finally, my thanks to the many coeliacs for their grateful enthusiasm and appreciation that has been the source of my inspiration for devising new recipes.

Joan Noble